THE BIGFOOT

VOLUME ONE

MICHAEL W. COOK

HANGAR 1 PUBLISHING

To all the intrepid researchers, both amateur and professional, who dedicate their time, energy, and passion to the pursuit of truth, even when that truth remains elusive. This book is a testament to your unwavering dedication to unraveling the mysteries that surround us, and to the pursuit of knowledge, even in the face of skepticism and doubt. Your perseverance inspires me, and it is my sincere hope that this work contributes, in some small way, to furthering our understanding of this enduring enigma. It is dedicated to those who dare to explore the shadows where science meets the unknown and embrace the wonder of the unexplored wilderness, for it is within those spaces that the most extraordinary discoveries are often made. This book is also a dedication to the indigenous communities whose oral histories and traditional knowledge hold the key to unlocking many of the secrets of the natural world, and whose deep connection to the land has sustained the lore of Sasquatch through generations.

For Roscoe, my best friend...

CONTENTS

PREFACE

The enigma of Sasquatch, or Bigfoot, has captivated the human imagination for generations. From whispered tales around ancient campfires to modern-day expeditions equipped with cutting-edge technology, the mystery surrounding this elusive creature continues to fuel debate, inspire research, and ignite the passions of countless individuals. This book doesn't claim to provide a definitive answer to the question of Bigfoot's existence. Rather, it serves as a comprehensive exploration of the subject, drawing upon historical accounts, scientific analysis, and the perspectives of key researchers. It acknowledges the inherent skepticism surrounding the topic while presenting a fair and balanced assessment of the evidence, encouraging readers to form their own conclusions. Throughout this journey, we will examine the various theories proposed, from folklore interpretations to more scientific hypotheses regarding the possibility of an undiscovered primate species. The book delves into the methodology employed by researchers, both past and present, highlighting the challenges and triumphs of their investigations. We'll analyze the credibility of various claims, scrutinize the physical evidence, and evaluate the potential impact of technological advancements on the future of Bigfoot research. This exploration is not simply a recounting of legends; it's an investigative journey into the heart of a complex and enduring mystery, one that demands critical thinking, respect for opposing viewpoints, and a deep appreciation for the boundless mysteries that still remain hidden within our world. Ultimately, the goal is to foster a richer understanding, encourage critical engagement with the evidence, and invite readers to participate in this ongoing conversation surrounding one of the world's most persistent and fascinating enigmas.

INTRODUCTION

For decades, the image of Sasquatch – a large, hairy bipedal creature inhabiting the remote forests of North America – has stirred both fervent belief and deep skepticism. This book embarks on a journey to navigate this complex terrain, seeking to offer a reasonable and thorough examination of the evidence and arguments surrounding this enduring mystery. We will traverse the historical landscape, tracing the evolution of the Bigfoot legend from its roots in indigenous folklore to its modern-day manifestation in popular culture. We will explore the plethora of alleged sightings, analyzing their strengths and weaknesses, acknowledging the potential for misidentification while recognizing the compelling nature of some accounts. The book will analyze the physical evidence – the footprints, hair samples, and purported vocalizations – subjecting them to rigorous scrutiny, examining the scientific methodologies used to evaluate their authenticity and the limitations inherent in such assessments. Central to this investigation is a profile of the key researchers, investigators, and scientists who have dedicated their lives to uncovering the truth behind the legend, highlighting their methodologies, the challenges they face, and their contributions to the ongoing discourse. We will also delve into the psychological aspects of belief and skepticism, examining the cognitive biases that may influence the interpretation of ambiguous evidence and exploring the potential for deliberate deception or misrepresentation. This investigation aims to provide a balanced perspective, recognizing the limitations of current evidence while acknowledging the possibility of a surprising reality. Finally, we will venture into the future, exploring the potential of advanced technologies – from genetic analysis to sophisticated imaging techniques – and considering how these tools might revolutionize our understanding of this enigmatic creature and its place within the natural world. This exploration is an invitation to engage critically with the available evidence, to consider multiple perspectives, and to participate in the ongoing quest to understand the enduring mystery of Sasquatch.

FOREWORD

GWENDOLYN PURCELL

I thought writing a forward to a book would be a lot easier than it turned out to be. I started over several times but finally managed to just be me. I never believed in Bigfoot. I never even gave it an ounce of thought. I guess you could say that I kinda thought all those people looking were just crazy and no such thing existed. Then, on a cold day in February, 2021, a creature I had never seen before walked into my life, literally. I tried for a while to justify what I saw, to try make it fit something else. At the end of the day, there was nothing I could put this image into. There was no box to throw it in. It was what it was, Bigfoot, and ever since then I have spent every waking moment with that big, hairy guy on my mind. I drive down the road and think, "he could be right there, watching as I pass." I have been called crazy. It's okay, I guess I am a little crazy. After all, I go to the woods, often in the pitch dark, chasing after a legend. But let's talk about all the things that Bigfoot has given me that I never had before and didn't know I needed.

Bigfoot gave me wings, so to speak. I grew up being told I was nothing and would never be anything. Bigfoot showed me that it doesn't matter what people think. It only matters what is inside my own head and heart. He taught me to be me, unapologetically. From the second I went down this rabbit hole, I began to meet people who believed in the creature. Some of these people have been chasing this legend far longer than I could have ever imagined. Some longer than I have been alive. I went on an expedition, deep into the Alleghany National Forest, with a group of seasoned researchers. My husband said I was crazy to pay that kind of money to go camping with a group of people I had never met. And maybe I was, but what I took from that trip was amazing. I met some of the best people I have ever met in my life. A few of these people I still research with today. I made lifelong friends. On that trip, Got Knockers was born.

Shortly after that expedition, I started to attend festivals and conferences. The first was in Virginia. I was super excited as this was not only my first Bigfoot festival, but also my first vendor event selling my brand of Bigfoot merchandise. The place was crowded and I was slowly making my way around the event when I came across this table where a guy was selling BBQ sauce. I was like 'OMGOSH, I saw that guy on a TV show I watched!' I tried very hard to keep cool and not spaz out. To my surprise, he was very nice, and we must have talked for an hour. I, of course, bought a bottle of every flavor of sauce he had. You may have guessed it, it was Michael Cook. Little did I know then, that day would start the formation of my extended family, what I call my Bigfoot family. Several years later, I would call Michael my brother, and I am closer with him than I am to my own family. I have a band of brothers and sisters that I would lay my life on the line for, and I know they feel the same about me. We all have this crazy life, a life built around a big, hairy, smelly, elusive creature named Bigfoot.

And I know you're probably thinking, what the hell does any of this have to do with what this book is about? What you will read in this book is very scientific. Michael dives into ALL the strange theories and mysteries. He looks at every side, every angle. This book is for everyone, not just the flesh and blood people or the interdimensional people or any other type of people. Bigfoot has given ALL of us something outside our normal, boring lives. Like any other group of people, there can be a lot of arguing and fighting. Some people are unable to have an open mind and only want to argue and fight about what Bigfoot is, in their opinion. I refuse to camp out in any of these camps. I refuse to conform to any one thought process until I find the proof of what Bigfoot is, or isn't. To be truthful, I am not sure I ever really want to know. I love a good mystery, and I love being in the woods, looking for the clues to solve a mystery. Even if the mystery gets solved, I think I will still be in the woods, looking, hoping, and waiting.

1

THE RIVERBANK

It was a beautiful, October morning in Southeastern Kentucky, I was 16 and had obtained my driver's license the month before. My parents would let me have a little more freedom than some 16-year old's out there, so that morning I decided to take a day off school to go fishing. Fishing was and has always been my favorite pastime, from the time I was born I had always been fishing. My parents took me on the boat in a baby carrier when I was just months old, so it's safe to say that I have had fishing in my blood my whole life. I would have never thought that fishing trip that day would change the course of my whole life.

I drove up to Martin's Fork Lake dam that morning and tried my hand at fishing in the impoundment at the dam, with no luck at all. I decided to drive down the road and try the river leading from the dam; I parked on the side of the road and took a short walk down to the riverbank. Almost instantly I realized I had made the right move, since I started getting bites right away. The first fish I caught was a nice little smallmouth, nothing to brag about, but a fish, nonetheless. After the first two or three small fish, catch and release, of course, I got a feeling of being watched. This was a feeling I was all too familiar with, being in the woods most of my life, there is always some critter watching you. This feeling was a little different, though. Not long after I got the feeling, I started hearing movement on the ridge across from me, rustling in the leaves. The way the sun was coming up, along with the fog, it was hard to see what was making the sounds, so I assumed it was squirrels playing, or maybe even a deer walking.

The rustling kept getting louder as it neared, but I still maintained it to be something like a deer or other small animal. I was in the middle of casting my line when a loud crash happened, followed by something coming down the hill at a high rate of speed. I reeled in quick to pay attention to what was going on. The crashing, grunting, and slapping sound ended as a large ball of fur rolled off the ledge of the bank into the river. My first thought was that it had to be a bear, so I laid down my gear to prepare to skedaddle in the event of a wet, possibly injured, pissed off bear springing out on my side of the river. After a few seconds passed, rising out of the water was something I had never witnessed before.

Standing around 8 feet tall, a large figure was holding up its arms and wading in chest-deep water towards the adjacent side. It reached up and grabbed ahold of a tree limb hanging off the bank and, in one stride, stepped up the 5-foot bank with ease. As it made its way towards sturdier ground, it began wringing the water from its long, soaked hair. The color of the fur was dark brown, almost black, but it was hard to tell since wet hair and fur takes on a darker look. I could clearly see its rough, weathered, black skin, and huge hands as it pushed the water from its fur, shaking as a dog would to rid itself of the excess water. This seemed to work for the creature, as the river water flicked and sprayed all around it like a shower. As the sun hit, its hair began to sheen, and I could see hints of brown and red coming through. The hair on its chest was shorter than in other places, such as the elbows, which had longer hair cascading off. The head was completely covered in a long mane of hair that flowed past its shoulders, parting at the face. The face itself possessed a high-cheeked beard, large flat nose, and deep-set eyes. From what I could see, the area around the eyes was free from hair. As it opened and shut its mouth, I could see large teeth.

Of all the details I recall from this incident, the one that stayed with me all these years has been its hands, more so the fingers. It had large hands, both with five distinct digits. This detail stood out, mainly because, at the time, I knew we, as primates, were the only animals on earth that had these features, along with our cousins in the primate species. Nevertheless, we were the only species in Eastern Kentucky to have these distinct features, or so I thought.

The creature began to ascend back up the ridge, as I stood there motionless watching its every move, then it stopped. When it stopped walking, it turned its head and looked back over its shoulder straight at me. It turned its whole body, to better stand on the steep embankment, and we stared at each other. The look on its face was much one of embarrassment, as though it was ashamed of itself for not only falling off the ridge, but for doing so right in the clear and present view of a human. As this mutual stare persisted, I tried mustering up enough to make a run for it; though my brain was screaming to run, my legs were not getting the message. The creature then let out a series of loud, aggressive grunts, while balling its fists. After the third or fourth grunt, my legs finally received the memo.

I ran as hard and as fast as I could, knowing for a fact that this monster had crossed the river and was right on my heels. I ran up the hill and charged into my car, screaming the whole time, as this creature was bound to rip the door off and drag me out, taking me into the woods to kill me. I frantically looked around, realizing that this monster had not followed or chased me, but now it was nowhere to be seen. As I began calming down, trying to regain my breath, I rolled down my window to let in some fresh air. From upon the ridge, a sharp, guttural, soul piercing scream came, and I quickly rolled the window back up and went back into panic mode. I could not have driven, I was shaking too much, so I just sat there listening to the screams from the ridge. After a few minutes passed, the screaming stopped. I sat there for a long time, watching the ridge line, something I feel was the first spark of curiosity born from fear. When I felt the moment was right, I made a mad dash to retrieve my gear from the riverbank. To this day, I strongly believe that was the world record 100 yard dash, and that I should've tried out for the Olympics.

Driving home, I knew what I was going to tell my parents, I knew that I had to tell them, I had to tell someone. Once I got home though, I was struck by a different fear. What if they didn't believe me? What if they thought I was crazy? As these thoughts came, I quickly decided to keep the incident to myself.

The next weeks and months became more and more difficult. The nightmares, the constant scanning of the woods, and the existential fear of going outside at night was becoming a clear problem.

Almost a year had passed, the stress, loss of sleep, and burden of the incident came to a head one night with my dad. We had sat down together to watch TV as one of our favorite shows was on. Unsolved Mysteries was a show about crimes, UFO encounters, missing persons, and unexplained events that had never been solved or explained. That night, the episode was about the legend of Bigfoot. As I watched, the video clips and interviews became all too familiar to me. I started flashing back to that day on the riverbank, and how these encounters were similar to what happened to me. Then the final clip was from a video shot in 1967, Bluff Creek, California, by Roger Patterson and Bob Gimlin, The Patterson-Gimlin footage; a video ridiculed by many but never explained with evidence of it being faked. I watched as the bigfoot on the clip turned its head and peered over its shoulder to look at the men filming it. The movement was remarkably similar to the one I saw made by the creature on the riverbank almost a year before. The color drained from my face as I broke out into a cold sweat, and my dad asked if I was okay.

I broke down and had to tell him everything, every detail about what happened the day I skipped school to go fishing. He listened intently as I told of the event and encounter, the nightmares, fear, and loss of sleep I had endured.

After I recalled everything to him, he nodded, closed his eyes, and sat there. I was expecting an outburst in laughter, I was expecting him to call me crazy, or say I was lying, but he never did any of that. He sat there for what seemed like forever when I finally yelled out. "Just tell me the truth!"

With a few words, the next 21 years would be set into motion, as he said, "I believe you, because They Are Out There..."

2

EARLY INDIGENOUS LEGENDS AND BIGFOOT MYTHOLOGY

L ong before the term "Bigfoot" entered the lexicon of modern cryptozoology, indigenous peoples across North America held rich oral traditions describing large, hairy bipedal creatures inhabiting the forests and mountains. These stories, passed down through generations, provide a crucial foundation for understanding the historical context of Bigfoot encounters. The descriptions and interpretations of these creatures vary significantly across different tribes and nations, reflecting the diverse cultural landscapes and beliefs systems of the indigenous populations.

For instance, among the Pacific Northwest Coast tribes, particularly those in the territories of present-day Washington, Oregon, and British Columbia, legends of a large, powerful being often associated with the wilderness are common. These stories frequently depict the creature as possessing immense strength and a connection to the spiritual world, sometimes acting as a guardian or trickster figure. Narratives often detail encounters that are neither wholly positive nor negative, but rather represent interactions within a complex ecosystem where humans and the spirit world coexist. These weren't simply tales of a monstrous beast, but stories intertwined with creation myths, moral lessons, and explanations of natural phenomena.

Detailed descriptions varied widely. Some accounts portrayed the creature as covered in dark, shaggy hair, while others described a more reddish or brownish hue. Its size, too, was a subject of variance across different oral histories, with some accounts suggesting a height comparable to an average human while others spoke of towering figures, easily surpassing seven feet in height. Regardless of the specific physical attributes, however, the common thread in these legends is a being of extraordinary power and mystery, deeply integrated into the spiritual fabric of these communities. Many legends emphasized a respect for the creature, warning against disturbing its habitat or provoking its ire.

Moving eastward, across the vast territories of the northern United States and Canada, Algonquian-speaking peoples, such as the Ojibwe and Cree, also possessed their own variations of these tales. Here, the creatures were often described as being more solitary and reclusive, often associated with remote, forested areas. The Algonquian tales tended to emphasize the creature's wildness and untamed nature, often portraying it as a powerful force beyond the control of humans. These accounts frequently emphasized the creature's elusiveness and its ability to disappear swiftly into the dense undergrowth.

The importance of understanding these diverse narratives cannot be overstated. These were not simply fanciful stories; they were integral parts of the cultures that transmitted them, shaping perspectives on the environment, spirituality, and the place of humans within the broader ecological system. To dismiss these accounts simply as folklore fails to recognize their enduring cultural significance and the profound knowledge they hold about the relationship between humanity and the natural world. Studying these stories is not only essential for understanding the history of Bigfoot beliefs but they also offer a window into the rich tapestry of indigenous cultures and their unique perspectives on the creatures that shared their world.

Beyond the oral traditions, we must consider the potential for a

blurring of lines between actual encounters and mythological interpretations. Did early indigenous peoples distinguish between sightings of unusual animals or hominids and their established mythical
beings? Did subsequent generations meld real observations with the
existing lore, gradually shaping the image of Sasquatch into a blend
of fact and fiction? These questions lack definitive answers, highlighting the challenges inherent in disentangling legend from
possible reality.

The absence of written documentation for many of these indigenous legends creates additional complexity. Oral histories, while
valuable, are susceptible to variations and interpretations over time.
The potential for distortion, loss of detail, or the blending of separate
narratives across generations presents a significant hurdle for
researchers attempting to reconstruct a clear picture of early indigenous beliefs about Bigfoot-like creatures. The limited number of
surviving accounts and the fragmented nature of available documentation often hinders comprehensive comparative analysis.

However, anthropological research and collaboration with indigenous communities are progressively filling in some of these gaps.
Efforts to meticulously document and analyze existing oral traditions, coupled with the growing respect for indigenous knowledge
systems, are leading to a more nuanced understanding of these early
legends. Modern researchers are increasingly working in collaboration with tribal elders and community members, recognizing the
value of their expertise and the essential role they play in preserving
and interpreting their ancestral knowledge. This collaborative
approach promises to provide invaluable insights into the origins of
Bigfoot mythology and shed light on the complex relationship
between humans, the environment, and the enduring mystery of the
Sasquatch.

The continued efforts to understand and contextualize these
indigenous legends are critical not only for enriching our knowledge
of Bigfoot, but also for promoting cross-cultural understanding and
the preservation of rich, ancient traditions. The narratives are not
merely historical artifacts; they hold the keys to understanding a

multifaceted aspect of human-nature interaction, offering insight into perceptions of the wilderness, spiritual beliefs, and ecological knowledge from perspectives too often overlooked or misinterpreted. By actively engaging with these rich cultural traditions, we can move beyond simplistic narratives and gain a far deeper appreciation for the complex origins of the Bigfoot legend. The task is not just to find Bigfoot, but also to appreciate the long-standing relationship between humans and the environment as it's reflected in these compelling and enduring stories.

The intertwining of fact and fiction in the Bigfoot narrative makes the task of separating the wheat from the chaff particularly challenging. Many accounts, though seemingly credible to the individual observers, lack the scientific rigor needed for objective validation. The inherent subjectivity of eyewitness testimony, coupled with potential for misidentification or exaggeration, necessitates a careful, critical approach to evaluating the credibility of various claims. The absence of robust, independently verifiable evidence further complicates the matter, leaving many accounts shrouded in ambiguity and speculation. This, however, does not diminish the importance of these indigenous legends, for they represent a crucial, foundational layer in the long and complex history of the Bigfoot phenomenon. Their continued study offers a profound window into the human relationship with the natural world, providing valuable insights into cultural beliefs, ecological understanding, and the enduring power of storytelling.

The impact of these early indigenous legends extends far beyond mere anecdotal evidence. These stories served as powerful tools for shaping societal behaviors, cultural values, and ecological stewardship. The depiction of Sasquatch as a powerful, sometimes dangerous, but ultimately integral part of the natural world encouraged a sense of respect for the wilderness and fostered a harmonious relationship between humans and their environment. Tales of consequences for those who disturbed Sasquatch's habitat or disrespected its power instilled caution and reinforced the importance of living in balance with nature. These lessons, encoded within these ancient stories, offer valuable perspectives on sustainable living and ecological consciousness, themes that resonate even more strongly in the context of modern environmental challenges.

Furthermore, the very existence of these consistent narratives across disparate indigenous groups suggests something more than simple coincidence. The recurrence of similar themes and descriptions across vast geographic areas and culturally distinct tribes raises the possibility of a common, underlying source for these legends. Were these consistent stories a result of actual encounters with an unusual creature, or did a common cultural archetype, perhaps reflecting a shared subconscious understanding of the wilderness, give rise to similar narratives across different groups? This question remains a central challenge in the quest to understand the origins and nature of the Sasquatch legend, highlighting the intertwining of anthropological, zoological, and psychological aspects of the phenomenon. The task, therefore, is not simply to dismiss these narratives as folklore, but to approach them as valuable sources of information, requiring careful analysis, critical examination, and a healthy dose of respectful humility.

The investigation of the Bigfoot phenomenon is not merely a quest to prove or disprove the existence of a single creature. It is a multi-faceted exploration of the intersection of anthropology, zoology, psychology, and cultural history. The study of indigenous legends forms a vital cornerstone of this investigation, offering a unique perspective on the longstanding human relationship with the mysterious world of wilderness and its potential inhabitants. The enduring power of these narratives testifies to the deep-seated human fascination with the unknown, a fascination that fuels the continued search for the elusive Sasquatch and inspires a deeper understanding of both our cultural heritage and the complex ecology of our planet. The journey to understanding the Bigfoot legend is, therefore, a journey through time, culture, and the enduring mystery of the natural world.

3

EARLY EUROPEAN ACCOUNTS AND THE GENESIS OF THE MODERN BIGFOOT LEGEND

The transition from indigenous oral traditions to documented European accounts marks a critical shift in the Bigfoot narrative. While Native American stories provided a rich tapestry of descriptions and beliefs, the arrival of European explorers and settlers introduced a new lens through which these encounters were interpreted and recorded. These early accounts, often filtered through the biases and preconceptions of the observers, laid the groundwork for the modern Bigfoot legend as we know it, a legend shaped by both genuine observations and the fertile ground of speculation.

Early explorers' journals and correspondence rarely mention creatures explicitly matching the modern Bigfoot description. This is not surprising; their primary concerns were survival, navigation, and the establishment of settlements, often leaving little time for meticulous documentation of unusual wildlife sightings. However, scattered references to large, hairy, human-like creatures appear within the broader context of their narratives. These accounts often lack the detail and specificity we expect from modern eyewitness testimonies, yet they hold a certain historical value as early glimpses into the developing perception of these elusive beings.

For instance, accounts from early fur trappers and mountain men in the Pacific Northwest occasionally allude to encounters with exceptionally large, bipedal primates. The vastness of the wilderness, the inherent dangers of their profession, and the lack of a standardized system for documenting unusual wildlife encounters mean these accounts are often fragmentary and anecdotal. Furthermore, the cultural context of the time is crucial. In a world where belief in mythical creatures and folklore was commonplace, reports of unusual animals might have been explained through the lens of existing superstitions or interpreted through the cultural framework of the times. This often led to a blending of potential observation with established mythology, obscuring the line between reality and folklore.

One example is found in the writings of explorers venturing into the mountainous regions of what is now the western United States. While their primary focus remained on mapping territories and establishing trade routes, some passages hint at encounters with creatures exceeding normal human size and exhibiting unusual physical characteristics. Often these were quickly dismissed as exaggerated tales or folklore, but their existence in historical documents provides a link between the indigenous oral histories and the later more focused investigations of the 20th century. The vagueness of these early accounts stems not only from the limitations of observation but also from the inherent skepticism with which such unusual claims would have been met in the broader scientific and societal context.

The 19th century saw a gradual shift towards a more scientific approach to natural history, but the exploration of remote wilderness areas remained a challenging and often dangerous undertaking. As scientific expeditions ventured further into unexplored territories, their detailed records and observations offered greater scope for documenting unusual wildlife encounters. However, these records often lack the consistency and rigorous methodologies employed in modern cryptozoological investigations.

The interpretations of these early observations were heavily influenced by prevailing cultural beliefs and the limited understanding of primate evolution and diversity. For instance, reports of giant apes in unexplored regions might have been interpreted through the lens of existing myths and legends, or attributed to known species exhibiting unusual variations in size or morphology. The absence of clear photographic or skeletal evidence left ample room for interpretation and fueled the blending of fact and folklore. The lack of sophisticated scientific tools and techniques further complicated the assessment of such claims.

The increasing popularity of frontier literature and tall tales in the 19th century further complicated the understanding of early Bigfoot reports. Often these stories exaggerated encounters for dramatic effect or incorporated elements of folklore, creating a blurring of lines between genuine observation and fanciful storytelling. The very nature of oral storytelling, where accounts evolved and changed over time, contributed to this phenomenon.

The late 19th and early 20th centuries saw the rise of professional anthropologists and zoologists who began systematically documenting and studying indigenous cultures and wildlife. However, the Bigfoot legend remained largely confined to the fringes of scientific inquiry, treated more as an interesting folklore element than a subject worthy of rigorous investigation. This was partly due to a prevailing scientific skepticism, but also because of the difficulties inherent in investigating a creature so elusive and with such scant evidence. The lack of standardized methodologies and the relatively undeveloped state of primate taxonomy limited the ability of scientists to critically analyze early accounts.

It wasn't until the mid-20th century that the modern Bigfoot legend began to take shape. The confluence of factors – increased public awareness, the growing popularity of cryptozoology, and the availability of improved documentation techniques – contributed to a surge in reported sightings and a more concerted effort to investigate the phenomenon. However, the foundations of these modern investigations were built upon the early European accounts, often incomplete and filtered through the biases and limitations of their time.

Analyzing these early accounts requires a critical approach. We must consider the cultural context, the observer's biases, the limitations of their observation techniques, and the potential influence of folklore and storytelling. It's crucial to differentiate between genuine attempts at describing unusual wildlife encounters and embellished stories intended for entertainment or to convey a sense of the wilderness's untamed nature. The task is to sift through the historical layers of perception, separating the potentially genuine kernels of observation from the accumulated layers of myth and exaggeration.

The evolution of the Bigfoot legend from these early accounts demonstrates the complexities of interpreting historical evidence. The lack of rigorous scientific methodology in early reporting makes definitive conclusions difficult. However, by carefully examining the available historical data, we can trace the development of the Bigfoot narrative, understanding how it transitioned from ambiguous mentions in explorers' journals to the widely recognized legend of today. This historical analysis is fundamental to a balanced and nuanced understanding of the Bigfoot phenomenon, acknowledging the limitations of historical evidence while recognizing its value in illuminating the journey of this enduring mystery. The journey towards understanding the Bigfoot legend is inextricably linked to understanding how the very nature of its narrative has been shaped, distorted, and refined through time, culture, and the ever-evolving perception of the wilderness. The early European accounts, though often fragmented and imprecise, provide a crucial link in this chain of evidence, allowing us to trace the genesis of a legend that continues to capture the imagination and inspire debate to this day. The next stage of this investigation requires analyzing the influence of these early accounts on the development of modern Bigfoot investigations and the shaping of the prevailing cultural narrative.

4

THE RISE OF BIGFOOT
INVESTIGATIONS

The early 20th century saw a subtle shift in the perception of Bigfoot, moving away from the realm of purely indigenous folklore and into the nascent field of cryptozoology. While anecdotal accounts continued to trickle in from remote logging camps and isolated communities, these stories often lacked the detailed documentation and corroborating evidence that would later characterize modern investigations. The lack of widespread media attention and the inherent skepticism surrounding such tales meant that Bigfoot remained largely confined to the periphery of public consciousness. However, the seeds of a more systematic approach to Bigfoot research were being sown. This period witnessed the slow but steady accumulation of eyewitness testimony, albeit often filtered through the lens of local legends and personal interpretations. The evolving narrative began to incorporate elements of scientific inquiry, however rudimentary, laying the groundwork for the more organized investigations that would define the latter half of the century.

The pivotal moment arguably arrived in the 1950s, a decade that witnessed a remarkable surge in public interest in Bigfoot. The now-famous Bluff Creek incident of 1958, involving the footprint discoveries of Jerry Crew and others, served as a catalyst. These large, seemingly non-human footprints sparked widespread media attention, propelling Bigfoot from a regional curiosity to a national phenomenon. Newspapers across the country picked up the story, and for the first time, Bigfoot became a topic of mainstream conversation. This media coverage, while sometimes sensationalized, played a crucial role in popularizing the Bigfoot legend and establishing it firmly in the public imagination. The Bluff Creek incident and its subsequent media frenzy marked a turning point, ushering in an era of more organized and dedicated Bigfoot investigations.

Following the initial wave of excitement surrounding the Bluff Creek findings, several dedicated researchers and investigators emerged, actively pursuing leads and documenting potential evidence. These early pioneers, often working independently, laid the groundwork for future collaborative efforts and contributed significantly to the development of investigative methodologies. Their efforts, however imperfect by modern standards, involved painstaking fieldwork, diligently interviewing eyewitnesses, and meticulously documenting potential physical evidence, even if the quality and reliability of said evidence remained questionable. This period witnessed the birth of a nascent field of inquiry, one that grappled with the challenges of separating genuine encounters from misidentification, hoax, and folklore. The lack of established scientific protocols and the absence of clear guidelines often led to inconsistencies in data collection and interpretation. However, it was during this time that the foundations for the more systematic and rigorous investigations of later decades were laid.

The 1960s and 70s witnessed a dramatic escalation in Bigfoot investigations. Improved technology, such as more advanced cameras and recording equipment, allowed researchers to gather more detailed evidence, albeit still largely circumstantial. The legendary Patterson-Gimlin film, shot in 1967, became the cornerstone of Bigfoot's visual representation, despite enduring controversy regarding its authenticity. Regardless of its veracity, the film fueled further interest and helped solidify Bigfoot's image in the public consciousness. The decades also witnessed the proliferation of expeditions, many of which were undertaken by dedicated teams of researchers employing increasingly sophisticated methodologies. These expeditions, often venturing into remote and challenging terrain, involved tracking, footprint analysis, and the careful collection of potential physical evidence such as hair and scat samples. However, the inherent difficulties of tracking a creature that is believed to be both elusive and intelligent, combined with the limitations of the available technology, meant that concrete evidence remained scarce. The analyses of these samples often led to inconclusive results, perpetuating the debate surrounding Bigfoot's existence. This era represented a significant step towards a more scientific approach, although the limitations of technology and the challenges inherent to fieldwork often hampered progress.

The late 20th century witnessed a gradual shift in the nature of Bigfoot research. The initial wave of enthusiasm, often characterized by a somewhat haphazard approach, gave way to a more structured and organized effort. The emergence of dedicated research organizations brought a greater degree of coordination and collaboration among investigators. These organizations adopted more rigorous methodologies, aiming to enhance the reliability and validity of their findings. The application of advanced technologies, such as improved camera traps, DNA analysis, and sophisticated tracking techniques, became increasingly prevalent, reflecting the evolving scientific landscape. However, these technological advancements did not definitively resolve the mystery. The challenges associated with Bigfoot's elusive nature persisted, leading to inconclusive results and ongoing debate. Even with improved technology, separating genuine sightings from hoaxes and misidentifications remained a significant challenge.

The development of improved methods of data analysis also played a significant role. This involved the use of statistical modeling to analyze the distribution of eyewitness accounts and footprint patterns, aiming to identify potential areas of concentration and refine search strategies. Additionally, the development of sophisticated audio recording techniques contributed to attempts to collect and analyze Bigfoot vocalizations. These audio recordings and their analyses fueled discussions regarding the creature's potential communication methods, further intensifying research efforts. The analysis of purported Bigfoot tracks also underwent a transformation, with researchers developing more refined methods for casting and analyzing footprints. These methods were often combined with geographic information systems (GIS) technology to map the distribution of these tracks and better understand the creature's potential range and movement patterns. However, even with these advancements, the lack of conclusive physical evidence continued to be a major stumbling block.

The late 20th century also witnessed a growing recognition of the need for interdisciplinary collaboration. Researchers from various fields, including zoology, anthropology, genetics, and forensic science, began to contribute their expertise, enriching the investigation with diverse perspectives and techniques. This collaborative approach aimed to bring a greater degree of scientific rigor to the investigation of the Bigfoot phenomenon. However, the skepticism from mainstream science remained a significant obstacle. The lack of conclusive proof, compounded by the potential for hoaxes and misidentification, made it difficult to gain acceptance within the scientific community. The scientific community, deeply rooted in evidence-based methodology, expressed its reservations about the quality and reliability of much of the accumulated evidence, prompting further refinements of investigation methodologies. This challenge of gaining scientific validation remains a significant hurdle in Bigfoot research.

The narrative of Bigfoot investigations in the 20th century is one of evolution, transitioning from sporadic and often anecdotal accounts to more organized and technologically advanced expeditions. It's a story of increasing collaboration, enhanced methodologies, and persistent challenges. The quest to find definitive proof has been hampered by factors such as the elusive nature of the creature, the challenges of fieldwork in remote environments, and the ever-present potential for human error, misidentification, and deliberate deception. The lack of universally accepted evidence continues to fuel the debate and controversy surrounding Bigfoot's existence. Yet, the persistence of dedicated investigators, driven by a fascination with the unknown and a commitment to unraveling this enduring mystery, continues to shape the ongoing narrative of Bigfoot. The legacy of their work forms the backdrop against which 21st-century investigations continue to unfold. The ongoing evolution of investigative techniques, fueled by advancing technology and interdisciplinary collaboration, holds the potential for future breakthroughs. However, the core challenge remains— reconciling the accumulated anecdotal and circumstantial evidence with the need for concrete scientific proof.

5

PATTERNS AND INCONSISTENCIES

The transition from anecdotal accounts to more structured investigations in the latter half of the 20th century brought with it a surge in reported Sasquatch sightings. These encounters, however, varied dramatically in their quality and the supporting evidence offered. Some were fleeting glimpses in the twilight, described with poetic license and fueled by the imagination. Others boasted more concrete details—footprints, vocalizations, and even alleged physical evidence. Analyzing these diverse reports reveals a complex interplay of potential truth, misidentification, and outright fabrication, underscoring the enduring challenge of verifying Sasquatch's existence.

One notable cluster of sightings emerged from Bluff Creek, California, in the 1950s and 60s. The area, characterized by its dense redwood forests and rugged terrain, became a focal point for Bigfoot enthusiasts and researchers alike. The accounts from this region often described a large, bipedal creature with exceptional size and strength, leaving behind incredibly large footprints. While some of these accounts are compelling, lacking corroborating physical evidence beyond casts and photographs that are often debated and dismissed as hoaxes or misrepresentations, the Bluff Creek sightings played a pivotal role in popularizing the Bigfoot legend, drawing significant media attention and contributing to the growing body of anecdotal evidence. The lack of conclusive proof, however, continues to fuel skepticism.

A different type of evidence surfaced in the Pacific Northwest, where numerous reports described encountering large, smelly creatures in forested areas. These accounts frequently mention unusual vocalizations – deep guttural roars, howls, and other sounds that deviate from known animal calls. Audio recordings from these encounters are often presented as supporting evidence. However, the challenges in authenticating such recordings are considerable. The possibility of natural sounds being misinterpreted or deliberate audio manipulation casts doubt on the validity of such evidence. Technological advancements in audio analysis could be instrumental in the future, but this technology was less refined in the past, making assessment more difficult.

Further complicating the analysis is the inherent variability in eyewitness accounts. Descriptions of Sasquatch's appearance vary widely, ranging from hairy bipeds with human-like features to more ape-like creatures. This lack of consistency poses a major hurdle in establishing a definitive physical profile. Factors such as lighting conditions, distance from the subject, personal biases, and the stress of encountering a potentially dangerous animal all contribute to variations in descriptions. Even the most credible witnesses sometimes provide conflicting details, suggesting the limits of human perception under challenging circumstances.

The analysis of alleged physical evidence, such as footprints, hair samples, and supposed remains, reveals similar patterns of inconsistency and uncertainty. While some casts of footprints have suggested enormous size and unusual gait patterns, many have been explained away by known animal tracks or human trickery. The challenges of accurately dating and verifying the origin of hair samples using earlier forensic techniques were significant. Many samples deemed to be Bigfoot have been identified as originating from known animals after more sophisticated testing. The lack of universally accepted protocols for analyzing this type of evidence further hampered attempts to reach conclusive findings. The absence of concrete skeletal remains, despite decades of searching, remains a major challenge to confirming the existence of Sasquatch.

Furthermore, the sheer remoteness of many purported Sasquatch habitats complicates investigation. The challenging terrain, often characterized by dense forests, rugged mountains, and unpredictable weather, renders many areas inaccessible. This inaccessibility presents difficulties in gathering credible evidence. The environmental conditions can compromise the integrity of potential evidence and hinder observation efforts.

Analyzing reported patterns in sightings reveals further challenges. Clusters of reports often appear in areas with a strong history of related folklore. This correlation suggests that cultural narratives may influence reported observations, leading to an enhanced likelihood of reported encounters, whether genuine or otherwise. This is not to say that every such sighting is entirely attributable to local folklore; however, it highlights the importance of carefully distinguishing between cultural influences and actual occurrences.

In evaluating the credibility of witnesses, investigators consider various factors, including their background, their past experiences, and their overall demeanor. Many witnesses are described as individuals with an established reputation for honesty and credibility. However, the subjective nature of eyewitness testimony continues to be a central challenge. The reliability of memories and the potential influence of suggestion and expectation make it difficult to separate truth from error. The pressure to provide compelling details – sometimes stemming from desire for fame, notoriety, or financial gain – can further influence the details of a reported sighting.

The photographic and video evidence presented over the years, while sometimes exciting, also bears careful scrutiny. The quality of early photographic and film evidence was often poor, making verification exceedingly difficult. Later, high-resolution images and videos may appear more credible but require careful analysis to rule out hoaxes, misidentifications, or the utilization of advanced techniques to create realistic yet misleading images or footage. The absence of clear and incontrovertible images remains a major obstacle in solidifying acceptance of Sasquatch's existence.

To summarize this complex area of study, the analysis of notable Sasquatch sightings in the 20th century reveals a fascinating, if frustrating, pattern of inconsistencies. While many reports claim compelling evidence—footprints, vocalizations, visual observations—the lack of universally accepted corroborating data, the difficulties in verifying eyewitness accounts and physical evidence, and the inherent challenges of fieldwork in remote locations make it impossible to draw definitive conclusions. The sheer volume of reports, coupled with the consistent lack of irrefutable proof, highlights the immense difficulties inherent in proving or disproving the existence of this elusive creature. The ongoing investigation into Bigfoot continues to be a balancing act between the accumulation of anecdotal and circumstantial evidence and the constant search for undeniable scientific proof. This ongoing debate highlights the limits of our understanding of the natural world and reminds us of the enduring power of mystery and the ongoing pursuit of the unknown. The legacy of the 20th century investigations serves as both a testament to human perseverance and a reminder of the enduring ambiguity surrounding the Bigfoot phenomenon. The next chapter will explore the ongoing evolution of Bigfoot research,

examining the technological advancements and new approaches that are shaping this area of inquiry.

6

A CRITICAL ASSESSMENT OF THE MOST FAMOUS EVIDENCE

The transition from the often-speculative accounts of the mid-20th century to the era of the Patterson-Gimlin film marks a pivotal moment in Bigfoot lore. Shot on October 20, 1967, in Bluff Creek, California, by Roger Patterson and Robert Gimlin, the film, a grainy 59-second sequence, purports to show a large, bipedal creature walking through a wooded area. Its immediate and lasting impact on the Bigfoot debate cannot be overstated. Prior to its release, Bigfoot sightings remained largely relegated to the realm of anecdotal evidence, dismissed by many as folklore or misinterpretations. The Patterson-Gimlin film, however, catapulted the subject into the mainstream consciousness, fueling intense speculation and igniting decades of debate regarding its authenticity.

The film itself depicts a creature of apparent significant size, covered in dark, shaggy hair, walking with a distinct gait. The creature's apparent anatomy—its size, musculature, and the way it moves—defies easy explanation. This seemingly tangible visual evidence, however flawed, immediately overshadowed previous accounts. The film's immediate impact was a surge in interest and investment in Bigfoot research. Expeditions to Bluff Creek increased dramatically, and researchers spent years attempting to corroborate the film's claims. Numerous expeditions revisited the area in search of additional evidence—footprints, scat, and other signs—but with limited success. Despite the lack of concrete further evidence directly linking to the film's subject, the footage itself became, and remains, the cornerstone of many believers' arguments.

However, from almost the moment of its release, the film's authenticity has been fiercely contested. Skeptics have pointed to various anomalies within the film itself to argue for its fabrication. One of the most frequently cited points of contention revolves around the creature's gait. While the creature's stride appears somewhat natural, some argue that the way the creature's apparent legs and arms move appears incongruous with established principles of bipedal locomotion. Detailed frame-by-frame analyses have been conducted, comparing the creature's movements to those of humans in similar costumes or even large apes. These analyses often point to discrepancies, suggesting the possibility of a hoax involving a person in a costume. Indeed, several individuals have come forward over the years claiming to have been involved in the creation of a hoax, although their accounts often conflict, and conclusive verification remains elusive.

The quality of the film itself adds another layer of complexity to the analysis. The grainy, shaky footage is far from the clear, high-definition images expected by modern standards. This poor quality fuels both arguments for and against authenticity. Proponents of the film argue that the conditions under which it was filmed—the dense forest, limited light, and the distance between the cameraperson and the subject—account for the poor quality. This suggests the footage is real and not professionally produced. Critics, however, posit that the poor quality aids in concealing a potential hoax, making it harder to definitively prove or disprove the true nature of the subject. They argue that any supposed anomalies or inconsistencies in the creature's anatomy could be easily hidden within the blurry frame.

Beyond the technical aspects of the film itself, the credibility of Patterson and Gimlin, the filmmakers, has also been scrutinized. While there has never been definitive proof of fabrication on their part, inconsistencies in their accounts and certain aspects of their behavior leading up to and after the filming have been questioned. The lack of further concrete evidence, such as photographs or additional footage, despite numerous subsequent expeditions to the same location, is also a point of contention.

The analysis of the Patterson-Gimlin film extends far beyond a simple yes or no answer to the question of its authenticity.

The film's longevity as a central piece of evidence in the Bigfoot debate lies in its unique position as a visually compelling piece of potential evidence. Even among the many skeptics, the film is acknowledged for its remarkable impact on the field and its ability to spark the imagination. The fact that it has survived decades of intense scrutiny and debate, undergoing countless analyses and interpretations, illustrates its remarkable power and enduring mystery.

Technological advancements have played a significant role in re-examining the footage over the years. Early analyses were limited by the available technology, focusing primarily on still frames and basic video analysis techniques. Modern techniques, such as advanced image enhancement and 3D modeling, offer a level of precision unimaginable in 1967. While these technologies have helped to address some of the ambiguities in the footage, they have also generated new avenues of debate and interpretation. For example, advanced image enhancement techniques might reveal details previously unseen, leading to further speculation about the creature's anatomy or providing additional evidence supporting or refuting the hoax theory.

The ongoing debate surrounding the Patterson-Gimlin film is not merely a scientific exercise; it is a cultural phenomenon. The film's enduring relevance stems from its ability to tap into our fascination with the unknown, our desire to believe in something larger than ourselves, and our inherent skepticism in the face of extraordinary claims. The film has become a symbol of the broader debate surrounding cryptozoology, representing the tension between faith and evidence, belief and skepticism. The debate surrounding its authenticity remains a crucial case study in the challenges of evaluating evidence related to paranormal phenomena, highlighting the difficulties in reconciling anecdotal accounts with the rigor of scientific inquiry. The lack of a definitive conclusion reinforces the persistent mystery surrounding Bigfoot and the enduring appeal of the unknown.

One cannot ignore the social and psychological aspects of the Patterson-Gimlin film's influence. It has become a defining image in the Bigfoot mythology, shaping how many people visualize the creature. Its impact extends beyond the realm of scientific inquiry, permeating popular culture and inspiring countless books, documentaries, and fictional works. The film's cultural significance, whether or not it proves genuine, is undeniable. It has captured the public imagination, fueling the mythos of Bigfoot for over five decades. It has, regardless of its true nature, become iconic.

The Patterson-Gimlin film's impact on Bigfoot research is multifaceted. While initially boosting interest and funding, the lack of conclusive evidence derived from the film itself has also led to criticism of the field. Some argue that the overemphasis on the film, coupled with the absence of further corroborating evidence, has diverted resources from other, potentially more fruitful avenues of investigation. This points to a broader issue within cryptozoology: the potential for captivating, but ultimately inconclusive, evidence to dominate the narrative, overshadowing other lines of inquiry.

Moreover, the film has raised fundamental questions about the nature of evidence itself. The difficulty in definitively proving or disproving its authenticity highlights the limitations of visual evidence, particularly in situations where the subject is elusive, the recording conditions are less than ideal, and the timeframe is relatively short. The film acts as a cautionary tale, demonstrating how even seemingly compelling visual evidence can be subject to interpretation and debate, and how easily misinterpretations can propagate. It illustrates the need for robust methodologies, incorporating multiple lines of evidence—including genetic material, vocalizations, and ecological data—for a more comprehensive understanding of any creature. This aspect of the film's legacy should not be underestimated; it serves as a valuable case study in the limitations of relying solely on visual evidence in the investigation of controversial subjects.

In conclusion, the Patterson-Gimlin film remains a controversial and fascinating piece of evidence in the Bigfoot debate. Its enduring impact lies not just in its visual content but also in its reflection of the broader challenges inherent in investigating cryptozoological phenomena. The film's ambiguity continues to fuel discussion, highlighting the persistent gaps in our understanding of the natural world and the limitations of our scientific tools and methodologies. It serves as a reminder of the power of mystery and our ongoing quest to uncover the truth, even when that truth remains elusive. Whether one believes in its authenticity or not, the film undeniably holds a significant place in the history of Bigfoot research, a testament to the enduring allure of the unknown and the compelling nature of a persistent mystery. Its legacy will likely continue to fascinate and challenge generations of cryptozoologists and researchers for years to come.

7

SIZE SHAPE AND GEOLOGICAL CONTEXT

Footprints, those fleeting impressions left in mud, snow, or sand, represent a cornerstone of Bigfoot evidence. While often dismissed as misidentifications or hoaxes, a careful analysis of footprint characteristics, coupled with an understanding of geological context, can reveal surprising insights. The sheer size of some alleged Bigfoot prints—far exceeding the dimensions of any known primate — immediately captures the attention. Prints measuring 15 inches or more in length, with widths proportionate to their length, challenge conventional understanding of primate anatomy. However, simply noting the size isn't sufficient; meticulous documentation and analysis are crucial.

The shape of the footprint itself offers further clues. While described as being similar to a human footprint, subtle differences have been noted. The lack of a distinct arch, a more elongated heel, and unusually spaced toes are among the frequently cited deviations. Furthermore, the presence of deep impressions, suggesting substantial weight and pressure, adds another layer of complexity. Examining the depth and clarity of the impression within its geological context becomes paramount. Soft mud yields a deeper, more detailed print than hard-packed earth or sand. The surrounding terrain can also reveal insights into the creature's gait and speed. The angle of approach and the presence of any accompanying tracks (e.g., drag marks from vegetation) can provide additional context.

Scientific approaches to footprint analysis incorporate multiple disciplines. Photogrammetry, a technique used to create three-dimensional models from two-dimensional photographs, allows for precise measurements and detailed analyses of the print's shape and depth. This allows researchers to compare the footprint to known animal tracks, further assessing the likelihood of misidentification. Geologists play a vital role in determining the age and authenticity of the footprint. Analysis of the soil strata surrounding the print can help estimate its age through dating techniques. This allows researchers to ascertain if the print was recently made or if it's an artifact of a much older event. The composition of the soil itself can reveal additional information, including the moisture content at the time the print was made, providing clues about environmental conditions.

One of the persistent challenges in footprint analysis stems from the inherent difficulties in preservation. Footprints are inherently ephemeral; they're susceptible to natural degradation from weather, erosion, and animal activity. Even the most careful documentation may not capture all the crucial details. The process of casting a footprint, often using plaster of Paris or other casting materials, introduces its own set of potential biases. The casting material itself may alter the original shape of the print, and the process can be disruptive to the surrounding geological context, hindering subsequent analysis. Therefore, photographic and video documentation, complemented by detailed field notes that include precise geographic coordinates, compass bearings, and environmental details, are vital in building a robust dataset.

The debate surrounding the authenticity of Bigfoot footprints is complex and often fraught with controversy. Critics often point to the lack of consistently verifiable evidence, citing the potential for human fabrication or the misidentification of known animal tracks.

However, proponents highlight instances of multiple tracks found over wide areas, spanning diverse terrains. These "trackways," as they are known, are cited as less easily explained by hoaxes or misidentification, suggesting coordinated movement over a considerable distance. Even so, the absence of clear video or photographic evidence of the creature making the prints continues to fuel skepticism. The transient nature of the footprints and the often remote and challenging environments where they are found make securing definitive proof incredibly difficult.

Beyond the individual footprint, the broader geographical distribution of purported Bigfoot prints also provides valuable data. The widespread geographic locations associated with these prints, ranging from the Pacific Northwest of North America to parts of Asia, challenge the notion that they are all easily explained away as local anomalies or misidentifications. The consistency in the general size and characteristics of these prints across large distances and vastly different terrains is noteworthy, demanding consideration. However, it also necessitates careful assessment to account for the potential for localized cultural influences and shared storytelling traditions that may contribute to consistent yet potentially inaccurate descriptions.

Furthermore, the geological context plays a crucial role in assessing footprint validity. For instance, footprints discovered in regions with consistent geological formations, demonstrating specific characteristics that are consistently repeated in multiple areas, hold greater weight. Conversely, footprints found in isolated instances or locations with unusual geological features require closer scrutiny. The study of the geological formation's stability and the footprint's embedding within that formation further supports or refutes the legitimacy of the discovery. If the geological formation itself is deemed unstable, it is more likely that the footprint could be the result of recent weathering or erosion, or possibly even a deliberate hoax designed to take advantage of an unstable geological setting.

The challenge in studying footprints is not simply their size and shape, but the difficulty in separating genuine occurrences from fabrications, mistakes, and natural phenomena. Some footprints attributed to Bigfoot have been convincingly shown to be fabricated, often for financial gain or local publicity. Others are the result of misidentification, stemming from a lack of experience in recognizing the footprints of various animals under diverse circumstances. For example, bear tracks, particularly those of large grizzlies, can sometimes be mistaken for Bigfoot prints due to their size and claw marks, though often lacking the distinctive, human-like features sometimes attributed to Bigfoot. Similarly, the tracks of other large animals such as moose or elk, when viewed in unfavorable lighting conditions or from a distance, can be misinterpreted.

To mitigate the potential for error, rigorous methodologies are essential. Footprint analysis shouldn't rely solely on visual inspection. Precise measurements, casting techniques, and careful documentation—including photographic evidence from multiple angles, GPS coordinates, and detailed descriptions of the surrounding terrain—are all crucial. The integration of multiple disciplines, such as geology and zoology, also helps to ensure a more thorough and objective assessment. Statistical analysis of multiple footprint findings can further identify patterns and similarities, strengthening the weight of evidence. The use of statistical analysis allows researchers to eliminate outliers or inconsistencies that could stem from misidentification or fabrication, providing a more accurate assessment of what the data suggests.

In conclusion, while footprint evidence remains highly debated in the context of Bigfoot research, sophisticated and rigorous analytical methods can help to separate credible evidence from speculation and error. By integrating multiple disciplines, embracing advanced techniques like photogrammetry, and adopting strict protocols for documentation and analysis, researchers can significantly enhance the scientific validity of footprint evidence. However, even with the most rigorous approaches, the elusive nature of the subject and the inherent difficulties in preserving and verifying footprint evidence mean that conclusive proof remains elusive. The continued development and application of innovative methodologies are crucial for advancing our understanding of this intriguing aspect of Bigfoot research. The scientific community must remain open to exploring all forms of evidence while maintaining a steadfast commitment to rigorous methodology and objective analysis. Only through a balanced and critically assessed approach can we hope to unravel the mystery surrounding these enigmatic footprints.

8

GENETIC TESTING AND CHALLENGES

The tantalizing possibility of obtaining definitive genetic proof of Bigfoot's existence rests heavily on the analysis of purported hair and tissue samples. Numerous samples have been presented over the years, ranging from single strands of hair found clinging to vegetation to larger clumps collected near alleged sighting locations. These samples, often accompanied by compelling eyewitness testimonies, have ignited hopes among researchers that genetic sequencing could finally provide irrefutable evidence. However, the reality is far more complex and challenging than a simple DNA test.

The initial hurdle lies in the authentication of the samples. Establishing a verifiable chain of custody is paramount. A sample's origin must be meticulously documented, ensuring that there is no possibility of contamination or substitution. Without a clear and unbroken chain of custody, the credibility of any subsequent genetic analysis is severely compromised. This is especially difficult in the context of Bigfoot research, where the encounters are often clandestine and the locations remote. The passage of time between sample collection and testing also presents a significant challenge; degradation of DNA can render analysis inconclusive or even impossible.

Once the authenticity of a sample is established (as far as possible), the actual genetic testing begins. This process requires sophisticated laboratory techniques and highly specialized expertise. The DNA extraction process itself is delicate; the sample must be handled with extreme care to avoid contamination. Even minute traces of human DNA can lead to misleading results. The extraction process often involves multiple steps, from the initial preparation of the sample to the amplification of the extracted DNA using polymerase chain reaction (PCR). The PCR process multiplies the DNA fragments, making it easier to analyze them.

The amplified DNA is then subjected to sequencing. This involves determining the exact order of nucleotide bases (adenine, guanine, cytosine, and thymine) within the DNA molecule. The sequence data is then compared to existing databases of known species. This is where the challenges become particularly pronounced. If the purported Bigfoot DNA is from an unknown species, as some researchers suspect, it might not show a clear match to any known organism in the current databases. This does not necessarily mean that the sample is a hoax, rather it highlights the limitations of our current understanding of biodiversity. The genetic landscape of the planet is vast and still largely unexplored. It's conceivable that the DNA from a Bigfoot sample could represent a creature outside the scope of our current databases, thereby highlighting the potential limits of current DNA analysis methods.

Furthermore, the interpretation of genetic data requires a high degree of expertise. Even with a perfectly sequenced genome, determining the phylogenetic relationship of an unknown species can be a complex undertaking. There is no single definitive test; researchers rely on a combination of approaches, comparing various genetic markers to infer relationships across different species. The analysis involves sophisticated bioinformatics tools and statistical modeling, requiring a high level of expertise in evolutionary biology and genomics. It is not unusual for researchers to disagree on the interpretation of genetic data, particularly in such ambiguous scenarios.

The quality of the genetic material itself plays a significant role in the success or failure of genetic analysis. Degraded DNA, often found in older or poorly preserved samples, can make sequencing extremely challenging. The amount of DNA extracted from a hair sample is typically small, making amplification crucial but also susceptible to contamination and error amplification. The presence of inhibitors in the sample, substances that interfere with the PCR process, can further hamper the analysis. Overcoming these challenges requires rigorous experimental design, meticulous laboratory procedures, and expert interpretation of the results.

The difficulties in obtaining conclusive results from hair and tissue samples are compounded by the possibility of deliberate hoaxes. Over the years, numerous purported Bigfoot samples have been exposed as fabrications, using animal hairs or other materials disguised as Bigfoot remains. Identifying these fraudulent samples requires careful microscopic examination, isotopic analysis, and sophisticated forensic techniques. Determining the age of a hair sample can be a particularly difficult undertaking, requiring expertise in various dating methods, such as radiocarbon dating, which can be used for older samples. This is, of course, particularly challenging with samples lacking an unbroken chain of custody.

Another aspect of the difficulty of Bigfoot hair and tissue analysis relates to the lack of a large number of verified and independently obtained samples. Unlike established species, where researchers have access to numerous specimens, the available purported Bigfoot samples are remarkably few and far between. This limited sample size hampers any attempts at establishing robust statistical analysis, making it difficult to draw definitive conclusions. A larger sample size would allow researchers to investigate the genetic diversity within the purported Bigfoot population, if it indeed exists, and further strengthen their analyses. This paucity of verified specimens necessitates a highly cautious and methodical approach to the interpretation of any existing data. The small number of samples also increases the importance of rigorous quality control measures at each stage of the analysis process.

Furthermore, the environmental conditions in which samples are often found can present significant challenges. Exposure to the elements, particularly in humid or damp conditions, can accelerate the degradation of DNA, leading to fragmentation and making analysis nearly impossible. Similarly, contamination from microorganisms in the soil or surrounding environment can interfere with the DNA extraction and sequencing processes. Researchers need to employ specialized protocols to minimize the risk of contamination, including using sterile equipment and employing suitable DNA extraction techniques designed to remove inhibitors and minimize environmental DNA.

The ethical considerations surrounding the acquisition and testing of purported Bigfoot samples also warrant discussion. Respect for wildlife and the preservation of natural ecosystems must always remain paramount. Any acquisition of samples must be conducted in a manner that minimizes disturbance to the environment and respects any potential animal rights issues. Furthermore, all research must adhere to ethical guidelines and regulations, ensuring that procedures are conducted responsibly and transparently. The integrity of the research relies heavily on these ethical considerations, preventing any potential harm to the natural environment and avoiding practices that might lead to misrepresentation of the results. Clear and transparent documentation of the collection methods is therefore also essential to ensure the validity of the research.

In conclusion, while the analysis of purported Bigfoot hair and tissue samples holds the promise of delivering definitive genetic evidence, the realities of the field are complex and fraught with challenges. From the authentication of samples and the intricacies of genetic testing to the interpretation of results and the ethical considerations involved, this area of Bigfoot research requires rigorous methodology, specialized expertise, and a healthy dose of skepticism. While advances in genetic technology continually offer new possibilities, the elusive nature of the subject and the challenges of obtaining verifiable samples continue to hinder definitive conclusions. The continued pursuit of rigorous scientific methods, paired with a commitment to ethical practices, holds the best hope of ultimately unraveling this long-standing mystery. Until then, the genetic puzzle of Bigfoot remains largely unsolved, tantalizing researchers and enthusiasts alike.

9

ACOUSTIC ANALYSIS OF BIGFOOT CALLS

The pursuit of Bigfoot has naturally extended beyond the visual realm, delving into the auditory landscape. While blurry photographs and ambiguous footprints remain the cornerstone of much of the evidence, the potential for acoustic analysis to contribute to the Bigfoot enigma is significant. Numerous recordings exist, purportedly capturing the vocalizations of this elusive creature. These range from low, guttural growls and howls to high-pitched screams and whistles, each adding a layer of complexity to the overall investigation. The challenge, however, lies not just in the acquisition of these recordings but in their rigorous scientific analysis and interpretation. The acoustic environment in which these sounds are recorded is crucial. Background noise, from natural sources like wind, wildlife, and even human activity, can easily obscure or distort the sounds, making accurate analysis extremely difficult.

One of the earliest and perhaps most well-known examples of purported Bigfoot vocalizations comes from the Patterson-Gimlin film encounter in 1967. While primarily a visual record, some accompanying audio recordings were claimed to have captured sounds associated with the creature. However, the quality of these early recordings is often poor, hindered by the limitations of recording technology at the time and the often challenging environments in which the recordings were made. This lack of high-fidelity recordings makes detailed acoustic analysis challenging, raising questions about authenticity and the possibility of misidentification. Indeed, the possibility of hoax recordings, either intentional or unintentional, must always be carefully considered.

Modern technology has dramatically improved the capacity for high-quality audio capture. Researchers now employ sophisticated recording equipment, including directional microphones and parabolic reflectors, to minimize background noise and enhance the capture of sounds from specific directions. This advance allows for a more nuanced understanding of the acoustic characteristics of potential Bigfoot calls. However, even with improved technology, challenges persist. The vast and often remote locations where Bigfoot is reportedly sighted often present significant challenges for recording high-quality audio. The terrain, weather conditions, and natural ambient sounds can all interfere with the recording process. The elusive nature of the creature itself presents yet another hurdle; capturing clear audio requires proximity, something that is notoriously difficult to achieve with a creature so rarely seen.

The interpretation of Bigfoot vocalizations is further complicated by the lack of a baseline for comparison. Without known recordings of a captive Bigfoot, researchers are forced to rely on comparative analysis of other primate vocalizations. This methodology involves comparing the acoustic properties of purported Bigfoot calls to those of known animals, particularly primates. By examining features such as frequency, amplitude, and duration, researchers attempt to identify similarities or differences. However, this approach is inherently limited; the vocalizations of existing primates may not accurately reflect those of a species that has potentially evolved in isolation for centuries, if indeed Bigfoot exists as a separate species.

The acoustic analysis of purported Bigfoot calls has also employed advanced signal processing techniques, using sophisticated software to filter out background noise, isolate specific frequencies, and enhance the clarity of the recordings. These methods are borrowed from various fields, such as bioacoustics and forensic audio analysis. These techniques aim to isolate and highlight the potentially salient features of the vocalizations, offering a more objective and detailed analysis. However, the interpretation of these processed sounds still relies heavily on the expertise and judgment of the analysts.

A critical component of acoustic analysis is the consideration of contextual information. This includes details such as the location of the recording, the time of year, the environmental conditions, and any eyewitness accounts associated with the event. Understanding the circumstances under which the sounds were recorded is essential to evaluating their plausibility. For example, a low growl recorded near a riverbank at night might be more likely to be attributed to a large animal than a similar sound recorded in a densely populated area during the day.

Beyond individual calls, researchers also examine the broader soundscapes in which the recordings were made. By analyzing the entire acoustic environment, it is possible to identify additional clues, such as the presence or absence of other animal vocalizations, the types of environmental noises present, and the overall acoustic character of the area. This holistic approach can help to determine the context of the recording and provide further evidence for or against the possibility of Bigfoot vocalizations.

Another layer of complexity involves the potential for intentional mimicry or hoaxes. The deliberate creation of sounds intended to mimic Bigfoot vocalizations is a known phenomenon, presenting a significant challenge to researchers attempting to authenticate recordings. Sophisticated audio analysis techniques are often necessary to distinguish genuine sounds from fabricated ones. The use of spectral analysis and other sophisticated methods helps to identify artificial manipulations in the audio recordings. These techniques look for patterns and inconsistencies that might indicate a recording has been artificially modified or created.

The scientific community remains largely divided on the validity of purported Bigfoot vocalizations. Skeptics often point to the lack of clear, high-quality recordings, the potential for misidentification, and the possibility of hoax recordings. They argue that the existing evidence is insufficient to support claims of a unique and undiscovered primate species. Proponents, however, highlight the consistent reports of unusual sounds associated with Bigfoot sightings, the potential for advanced acoustic analysis to reveal subtle characteristics of the calls, and the possibility that these vocalizations may provide valuable insights into the behavior and social structure of Bigfoot, if it exists.

The ongoing debate highlights the need for continued rigorous research and the development of even more sophisticated analytical techniques. The collaboration between cryptozoologists, acousticians, and other experts is crucial to advance our understanding of the auditory evidence surrounding Bigfoot. Future investigations might benefit from the application of machine learning and artificial intelligence, which could potentially help to sift through vast amounts of audio data and identify patterns that may not be readily apparent to human analysts. The development of more advanced algorithms for noise reduction and sound source identification could also significantly improve the accuracy and reliability of acoustic analysis.

In conclusion, the analysis of purported Bigfoot vocalizations offers a fascinating, yet challenging, avenue of investigation. While the quality and authenticity of many existing recordings remain questionable, advancements in recording technology and acoustic analysis methods offer new possibilities for future research. The careful consideration of contextual information, the use of advanced signal processing techniques, and the collaborative efforts of experts across different disciplines are essential to determine the validity of these vocalizations and their potential contribution to our understanding of the Bigfoot enigma. The mystery continues, and the sounds of the wilderness hold both promise and uncertainty for those dedicated to unraveling its secrets. The future of acoustic analysis in Bigfoot research hinges upon a rigorous, scientific approach coupled with a willingness to embrace new technologies and collaborative investigation. Only then might we finally hope to separate the genuine from the spurious and draw closer to a conclusive answer.

10

UNUSUAL STRUCTURES ANOMALIES AND ARTIFACTS

Beyond the fleeting glimpses and ambiguous audio recordings, the search for physical evidence of Bigfoot often leads investigators down a path of intriguing, albeit often controversial, anomalies. The sheer size and purported strength attributed to the creature suggest the possibility of more substantial physical remnants – evidence that extends beyond fleeting footprints or strands of hair. This realm of investigation focuses on what we might term "unusual structures, anomalies, and artifacts." These are often the most debated pieces of evidence, prone to misinterpretations and lacking the definitive clarity of, say, a clear photographic capture. However, their existence warrants careful examination.

One of the most frequently cited pieces of potential physical evidence is the discovery of purported "Bigfoot nests." These are typically described as large, deeply recessed areas within dense forest cover, often containing broken branches, flattened vegetation, and sometimes even seemingly organized piles of debris. While many skeptics dismiss these formations as natural occurrences resulting from windstorms, animal activity, or even human interference, some researchers believe that they exhibit a degree of deliberate construction or organization not easily explained by natural processes. The scale of some of these structures— often significantly larger than those typically associated with known animals in the region—adds to the intrigue. For instance, accounts from the Pacific Northwest describe nests spanning several hundred square feet, featuring intricate arrangements of branches and vegetation, seemingly designed to provide shelter or concealment. However, the lack of consistent, verifiable characteristics across reported nests makes conclusive analysis difficult. The criteria for defining a "Bigfoot nest" is vague, leading to subjective interpretations and potential for bias in data collection. Detailed photographic documentation, precise mapping of the site, and comprehensive analysis of the vegetation and debris would be essential to establish the authenticity and significance of any purported nest. The absence of consistent and rigorous methodology in past investigations has significantly hampered the scientific evaluation of this type of evidence.

Another category of potential physical evidence involves unusual structures found within the alleged habitat of Bigfoot. These could include oddly shaped depressions in the ground, unusual groupings of rocks, or even patterns of broken branches suggesting deliberate manipulation. Some researchers propose that these structures might serve as marking points, territorial boundaries, or even crude communication tools. The interpretation of these features is highly dependent on context and requires careful consideration of alternative explanations. Geologic formations, animal burrows, and human activity can all mimic the appearance of artificial structures, making it crucial to eliminate these possibilities before ascribing them to Bigfoot. Again, rigorous documentation and comparative analysis are necessary to evaluate their significance. The absence of repeatable patterns or consistent characteristics across reported instances raises serious questions about their validity as evidence.

The reported discovery of unusual artifacts also falls within this category. These could range from large, unexplained footprints to purportedly unusual tools or implements found in remote areas. One example is the frequent reporting of exceptionally large footprints, exceeding the dimensions typically attributed to humans or other known animals.

While the possibility of hoaxing or misidentification is always present, some researchers argue that the sheer consistency of some footprint reports, particularly in specific regions, deserves further investigation. The challenge, however, lies in obtaining verifiable, unaltered casts or photographs of these prints. Many alleged casts have suffered from poor documentation, improper preservation, or even deliberate manipulation. Similarly, reports of large, broken branches or other materials exhibiting unusual characteristics raise questions. Analyzing the breakage patterns, the type of wood, and the surrounding environment could potentially reveal evidence of extraordinary strength or unusual manipulation—assuming, of course, that the artifacts themselves are authentic and have not been tampered with.

However, the inherent challenges in dealing with this type of evidence must be acknowledged. The lack of controlled observations, the potential for misinterpretation, and the prevalence of hoaxing have all contributed to skepticism surrounding these claims. Further-more, the difficulty in accessing remote locations, coupled with the inherent degradation of organic materials over time, adds further complexity. Many instances of purported Bigfoot evidence are lost to time, degradation, or a lack of proper preservation. Even the most meticulously documented case may become a subject of intense debate, due to the inherently subjective nature of the interpretation of ambiguous findings.

The importance of rigorous scientific methodology cannot be overstated. Any claims of unusual structures, anomalies, or artifacts should be subject to thorough investigation, employing established scientific techniques. This includes detailed photographic and video-graphic documentation, GPS mapping, 3D scanning, and laboratory analysis of any physical samples. Moreover, alternative explanations should be meticulously explored and ruled out before assigning any significance to the alleged evidence. A crucial component of this process involves careful consideration of the context— the geological features, the local fauna and flora, and even the history of human activity within the specific location. Understanding the natural processes at play in a given area is essential to eliminate potential misinterpretations and avoid confirmation bias.

The subjective nature of interpretation represents another significant hurdle. What one person perceives as an organized structure, another might dismiss as a random arrangement of natural debris. This inherent subjectivity highlights the need for standardized criteria and rigorous documentation to ensure consistency and minimize bias. This calls for a multi-disciplinary approach, bringing together experts from diverse fields like geology, botany, zoology, and anthropology. The collaborative analysis of evidence from multiple perspectives increases the chances of a more objective and comprehensive assessment.

Furthermore, the use of advanced technologies holds immense potential for future investigations. Techniques like LiDAR (Light Detection and Ranging) could be employed to create highly accurate 3D models of terrain, allowing for the precise mapping of unusual structures and anomalies. Advanced image analysis techniques can be employed to enhance low-quality photos and videos, and DNA analysis could potentially identify the source of any biological material found near the purported structures. The development of new non-invasive monitoring technologies, such as remote sensing cameras and acoustic monitoring systems, can provide continuous data collection without disturbing the environment or potentially influencing the behavior of any creature present.

In conclusion, the search for physical evidence beyond footprints and hair samples opens a complex and often contentious realm of investigation. While reports of unusual structures, anomalies, and artifacts contribute to the overall body of evidence surrounding Bigfoot, their interpretation and validation require rigorous scientific scrutiny. The subjective nature of this evidence, coupled with the challenges of accessing remote locations and the degradation of organic materials, necessitates a thorough, multidisciplinary approach that leverages both traditional investigative techniques and advanced technologies. Only through a dedicated and scientifically rigorous pursuit of this type of evidence can we hope to move closer to a more complete and objective understanding of the Bigfoot enigma. The future of this line of investigation hinges upon a commitment to objective analysis, collaborative research, and the application of cutting-edge technologies to unravel the secrets hidden within the wilderness. The path remains fraught with uncertainty, but the potential rewards for a better understanding of this persistent mystery are undeniable. The work continues, and the forests hold their secrets patiently.

11

CONTAMINATION AND MISIDENTIFICATION

T he pursuit of tangible evidence related to Bigfoot presents a formidable challenge, even surpassing the difficulties inherent in obtaining clear photographic or audio recordings. The ephemeral nature of many potential clues, coupled with the often remote and challenging environments where these creatures are purportedly sighted, introduces significant obstacles to evidence gathering and preservation. One of the most critical hurdles is contamination. Footprints, for example, are extremely vulnerable. Rain, snow, wind, animal activity, and even the passage of time itself can quickly obliterate subtle details, rendering them useless for analysis. The very act of approaching and documenting a footprint can introduce contamination, obscuring crucial characteristics like the depth of impression, the spacing and pattern of individual toes, or the unique features of the sole itself. Even seemingly innocuous actions, such as stepping near a footprint to take a photograph, can subtly alter its shape and potentially erase valuable data.

Similar problems arise with hair samples. The collection of hair must be conducted with extreme care to avoid contamination from human DNA or other environmental sources. Proper protocols require the use of sterile gloves and tools, along with meticulous documentation of the collection site, the surrounding environment, and any potential sources of contamination. Moreover, the degradation of hair over time is a significant factor. Exposure to sunlight, moisture, and microorganisms can rapidly break down the hair's structure, compromising its integrity and making DNA analysis difficult, if not impossible. The risk of cross-contamination is especially high if multiple samples are collected without stringent precautions, leading to a potential mix-up of genetic material and rendering the results meaningless.

Beyond footprints and hair, other potential forms of physical evidence, such as purported Bigfoot excrement or other organic matter, face even greater challenges in preservation. These materials are highly susceptible to decomposition and environmental degradation. The rate of decay is influenced by numerous factors, including temperature, humidity, and the presence of bacteria and insects. Without rapid and proper preservation techniques—such as freezing or chemical stabilization—these valuable samples can quickly deteriorate to the point where they become useless for analysis. The collection and handling of organic matter also requires specific protocols to minimize the risk of contamination with human DNA or other extraneous genetic material. Any contamination renders the sample's value virtually null, leading to wasted effort and potential misinterpretations.

Misidentification presents another major challenge in the analysis of physical evidence. Many purported Bigfoot tracks have been attributed to known animals, particularly bears. Bears, especially larger species like grizzly bears, can leave footprints that, under certain conditions, may superficially resemble those attributed to Bigfoot. The size and shape of the footprint are often the first indicators, but even these can be deceptive. The substrate—the ground itself—plays a crucial role. A soft, muddy surface can distort the true shape of a footprint, exaggerating its size and blurring its details. Conversely, a hard, dry surface may not fully register the full shape of the paw. Thus, discerning a genuine Bigfoot footprint from that of a bear, or another large animal, often requires careful consideration of the context, along with a detailed analysis of subtle features. For example, the presence of claw marks, the degree of heel impression, and the asymmetry of the footprint can all provide valuable information that helps distinguish between different species.

Similarly, hair samples can be easily misidentified. The microscopic analysis of hair shafts, including the examination of scales, medulla characteristics, and pigment distribution, is crucial for accurate species identification. However, even with microscopic analysis, misidentification is possible, particularly if the hair is degraded or if the analyst lacks sufficient expertise. Furthermore, the rarity of purported Bigfoot hair samples makes it incredibly difficult to establish definitive comparison points against established species reference collections. In fact, many such analyses conducted over the years have ultimately attributed claimed Bigfoot hairs to various other animals.

The challenges are compounded when considering the purported existence of unusual structures and artifacts associated with Bigfoot. Claims of unusual nests, large footprints on rock faces, or unexplained breakage of tree branches present distinct problems for evidence verification. These are often subjective observations, relying heavily on visual interpretation and photographic evidence, both of which are susceptible to various biases and manipulations. The lack of rigorous documentation and methodical analysis frequently undermines the credibility of such claims. Furthermore, the very remote nature of many locations where these structures and artifacts are supposedly found presents logistical problems in accessing, documenting, and properly analyzing them. Weather conditions, terrain difficulties, and lack of proper equipment can all severely hinder evidence gathering. The risk of altering or destroying the evidence during the process of documentation is high, further complicating matters.

Moreover, the lack of standardized protocols for the collection and analysis of Bigfoot-related evidence poses a significant challenge. In the absence of established guidelines, the quality and reliability of evidence varies considerably across different investigations. Different researchers employ diverse methodologies, potentially leading to inconsistencies and discrepancies in data interpretation. This variability makes it exceedingly difficult to compare and contrast results from multiple investigations, limiting the ability to draw conclusive inferences. The lack of a centralized database for Bigfoot evidence further exacerbates the problem, hindering the collaborative effort needed to advance the field.

The psychological factors also play a crucial role in the interpretation of evidence. The anticipation of encountering evidence of a legendary creature can significantly influence the observer's perceptions and interpretations. The phenomenon of pareidolia—the tendency to perceive meaningful patterns in random stimuli—is particularly relevant in this context. This can lead to misinterpretations of ambiguous features, causing observers to see Bigfoot characteristics in objects or phenomena that have alternative, more mundane explanations. Similarly, confirmation bias, the tendency to favor information that confirms existing beliefs, can lead researchers to interpret evidence selectively, reinforcing their preconceptions rather than objectively evaluating the available data. The inherent subjectivity involved in interpreting potentially ambiguous evidence calls for meticulous scrutiny and rigorous analytical techniques to mitigate these psychological biases.

In addition to the challenges described above, the ethical implications of Bigfoot research warrant careful consideration. The pursuit of evidence should always be conducted in a way that respects the environment and any potential wildlife present in the area. Unauthorized entry onto private lands, disturbance of wildlife habitats, and damage to natural resources are all unacceptable behaviors that undermine the credibility of the research and could have negative environmental consequences. Researchers have a responsibility to adhere to ethical guidelines and to prioritize the preservation of the natural world over their pursuit of evidence. Collaboration with relevant authorities, including land managers and environmental protection agencies, is crucial to ensure that research activities are conducted responsibly and legally. Transparent research methods and publicly available data are essential for building trust and ensuring the integrity of the scientific process.

The field of Bigfoot research continues to navigate a complex landscape of challenges in evidence gathering and preservation. Overcoming these hurdles requires a multidisciplinary approach that combines expertise in biology, genetics, anthropology, forensic science, and investigative journalism, among other fields. Furthermore, technological advancements could significantly contribute to resolving some of these issues. Improved DNA analysis techniques, for example, can provide more reliable species identification. Advanced imaging techniques could potentially enable more accurate and detailed documentation of footprints and other evidence. The development of remote sensing technologies, including motion-activated cameras and drones, offers opportunities for improved monitoring of potentially sensitive areas. However, even with these technological advancements, critical thinking, rigorous methodology, and a commitment to objective analysis remain paramount to unraveling the enduring mystery of Bigfoot. The path ahead is challenging but the potential rewards – a deeper understanding of our natural world and the enigmatic creatures that may inhabit it – are substantial, justifying the persistent and rigorous pursuit of evidence.

12

PROFILES OF LEADING BIGFOOT INVESTIGATORS

The pursuit of Bigfoot, a creature shrouded in mystery and legend, has attracted a diverse cast of researchers, each employing unique methodologies and contributing to the ongoing debate. Understanding their approaches is crucial to assessing the overall body of evidence and the credibility of various claims. While a definitive answer to Bigfoot's existence remains elusive, the work of these dedicated individuals has significantly shaped our understanding of the phenomenon.

Among the most prominent figures is Dr. Grover Krantz, a renowned anthropologist who dedicated a significant portion of his career to Bigfoot research. Krantz's methodology involved rigorous analysis of purported Bigfoot evidence, particularly footprints and skeletal remains. He was a staunch proponent of the undiscovered species hypothesis, arguing that the available evidence suggested a large, bipedal primate unknown to science. His meticulous examination of footprints, often utilizing sophisticated casting techniques and comparative analysis with known primate species, provided detailed insights into potential gait patterns and anatomical features. While his views weren't universally accepted within the scientific community, his dedication to meticulous analysis and his commitment to rigorous scientific methodology set a high standard for Bigfoot research. He was a vocal critic of what he considered sloppy or biased investigations, consistently pushing for more stringent evidentiary standards. His work, often controversial, generated considerable discussion and challenged prevailing assumptions. His legacy continues to inspire debate and rigorous approaches to the analysis of ambiguous evidence.

Another significant figure is Peter Byrne, a British journalist and author whose investigation delved deeply into the purported physical evidence associated with Bigfoot. Byrne's approach was characterized by a skeptical yet openminded perspective. He focused on a systematic review of available data, including footprint casts, hair samples, and eyewitness accounts. Unlike some researchers who might prioritize a singular theory, Byrne meticulously investigated different avenues of evidence, carefully weighing their strengths and weaknesses. His approach involved extensive fieldwork, involving direct contact with individuals who had claimed encounters with Bigfoot, meticulous documentation of their accounts, and thorough cross-referencing of information. He advocated for a multi-faceted approach, emphasizing the importance of considering alternative explanations, including misidentification and hoaxes, while remaining open to the possibility of an undiscovered species. His work served as a model for investigative journalism in the field of cryptozoology, emphasizing thorough research, critical analysis and balanced reporting. His deep skepticism was tempered by a rigorous search for verifiable data, making his work a cornerstone of the more scientifically minded approach to Bigfoot research.

Rene Dahinden, a Swiss researcher, took a strikingly different path. His approach emphasized the cultural and anthropological dimensions of the Bigfoot phenomenon. Dahinden's work focused on the pervasive nature of Bigfoot legends across various cultures and geographical locations. He posited that the existence of similar creatures in different folklore traditions worldwide might point to a deeper, potentially psychological, underpinning to the Bigfoot phenomenon rather than a purely biological one. His methodology centered on cross-cultural comparisons of Bigfoot-like legends, examining similarities and variations in descriptions, behaviors, and associated cultural beliefs. He analyzed the narratives, identifying recurring motifs and patterns that might reveal underlying archetypes or universal human anxieties projected onto a mysterious, powerful being inhabiting the wilderness. This approach contrasted sharply with the more biologically-focused research of others, highlighting the importance of considering the cultural and psychological contexts that shape our understanding of such phenomena. His work provided a valuable counterpoint to the predominantly biological approaches, enriching the understanding of the multi-faceted nature of Bigfoot's place in human culture.

Bob Heironimus, often associated with the Patterson-Gimlin film, represents a more controversial figure in Bigfoot research. While not a researcher in the traditional sense, his involvement with the film, its purported authenticity, and subsequent commentary has significantly influenced public perception. While some maintain the film depicts a genuine Bigfoot, others have pointed to evidence that suggests a hoax. The methodological approach to assessing the film's authenticity has involved detailed frame-by-frame analysis, employing techniques from image processing and biomechanics. The debate continues, but the controversy surrounding the film underscores the need for stringent analytical methods and a commitment to critical thinking in evaluating evidence. Heironimus's role highlights the complexities of evidence evaluation and the importance of distinguishing between genuine evidence and potentially misleading material.

Jeff Meldrum, a professor of anatomy and anthropology, represents a more scientifically rigorous approach to Bigfoot research. Unlike some investigators who rely heavily on anecdotal evidence, Meldrum focused on the analysis of physical evidence. His work centered on the purported Bigfoot footprints, using his anatomical expertise to assess their characteristics and potential origins. He applied rigorous scientific methodology, using comparative anatomy, biomechanics, and track analysis to evaluate the plausibility of the tracks originating from a known primate species. His findings, often published in peer-reviewed journals, have contributed to a more scientifically grounded understanding of the physical evidence. Meldrum's methodical approach has brought a level of scientific rigor often lacking in Bigfoot research, fostering a more measured and objective assessment of potential evidence.

These researchers, with their diverse methodologies and perspectives, illustrate the complexity of Bigfoot research. Their work, ranging from meticulous analysis of physical evidence to nuanced explorations of cultural narratives, contributes to a multi-faceted approach to understanding this enduring mystery. The ongoing debate highlights the challenges of investigating a creature that remains elusive and the importance of critical thinking and rigorous scientific inquiry. The future of Bigfoot research will likely involve a multidisciplinary approach, integrating insights from anthropology, biology, genetics, and technology, mirroring the varied approaches of the researchers profiled above. The continued dedication of these investigators, alongside advancements in technology and research methodologies, offers a glimmer of hope in unraveling the enigma of Bigfoot. The pursuit continues, driven by the enduring allure of the unknown and a commitment to unraveling one of nature's most enduring mysteries. Their combined efforts, despite differing conclusions, contribute significantly to a richer, more nuanced understanding of the phenomenon, underscoring the importance of diverse perspectives and a commitment to robust investigation in a field characterized by ambiguity and uncertainty. The legacy of these researchers is not merely the evidence they've gathered, but the standards of investigation they have set and the ongoing dialogue they've fostered within the field of cryptozoology.

13

TRACKING SURVEILLANCE AND DATA COLLECTION

The pursuit of evidence regarding Bigfoot necessitates a multifaceted approach, drawing on techniques honed over decades of investigation. While the elusive nature of the subject makes definitive proof challenging, rigorous methodology remains paramount. Tracking, surveillance, and meticulous data collection form the cornerstone of any credible Bigfoot investigation. These techniques, while seemingly straightforward, demand patience, expertise, and a keen eye for detail.

Tracking, often the initial phase of an investigation, relies heavily on the identification and interpretation of physical signs. Footprints, of course, are the most widely sought-after evidence. Experienced trackers assess not only the size and shape of the print, but also the depth of the impression, the substrate (type of soil, mud, snow), and the surrounding vegetation for signs of disturbance. The gait pattern, revealed by a series of prints, offers insights into the creature's size, weight, and even its possible locomotion style. Careful photography, using scales for accurate measurement and detailed notations of the surrounding environment, are crucial for preserving this evidence. Beyond footprints, investigators search for scat (feces), which can undergo genetic analysis to determine species. Similarly, hair samples, if found, represent a significant potential for DNA testing. Broken branches, disturbed undergrowth, and unusual formations in the terrain all contribute to a composite picture of the creature's movement and habitat. The art of tracking involves a combination of scientific observation and intuitive understanding of animal behavior, requiring years of experience and fieldcraft to master.

Surveillance, often employed after initial promising signs of activity are discovered, utilizes a range of technologies and strategies. Traditional methods include establishing observation points, employing camouflage, and using trail cameras. Trail cameras, motion-activated and strategically placed, have become increasingly valuable, allowing for passive monitoring over extended periods. Their cost-effectiveness and ability to capture images and video evidence without the need for constant human presence have revolutionized Bigfoot investigation. However, reliance on trail cameras alone is not sufficient. The potential for misidentification, including animal trickery, requires thorough scrutiny of all collected footage.

More sophisticated methods involve the use of acoustic monitoring devices, including high-sensitivity microphones and infrasound detectors. Infrasound, below the range of human hearing, is believed to be produced by certain animals and could potentially help in locating Bigfoot by detecting its low-frequency vocalizations. The strategic deployment of these technologies, often in conjunction with visual surveillance, maximizes the chances of capturing concrete evidence. The use of drones, equipped with high-resolution cameras and thermal imaging capabilities, is also gaining traction. Drones offer a unique perspective and can cover larger areas, increasing the search efficiency. However, their use must be carefully planned to avoid disturbing the environment and potentially scaring away the target. Ethical considerations concerning the use of drones are paramount; respecting wildlife and local regulations are essential for maintaining the integrity of the investigation.

Data collection is a critical phase that goes beyond simply gathering images or recordings. Each piece of evidence must be meticulously documented, including detailed geographical coordinates (ideally using GPS), timestamps, and descriptions of the surrounding environment. Precise measurements, photographic evidence with scales, and witness testimonies, if obtained, all form part of the comprehensive data set. The importance of minimizing bias in this process cannot be overstated. Each piece of evidence should be treated objectively, acknowledging the possibility of misidentification or alternative explanations. A rigorous chain of custody is essential to maintain the integrity of any physical evidence, preventing contamination or alteration. Detailed field notes, accurately recording all observations and methodologies, are fundamental to the reproducibility and subsequent scrutiny of the findings. These detailed records allow for rigorous analysis, comparative studies, and the identification of potential patterns or inconsistencies. Without meticulous record-keeping, the credibility of any findings is severely compromised.

Data analysis is the final, but equally crucial stage. This involves the careful scrutiny of all collected data, looking for patterns, correlations, and inconsistencies. Footprint analysis, for example, may involve comparing measurements to known animal prints and exploring variations in gait patterns. Acoustic recordings require sophisticated signal processing techniques to filter out noise and isolate potential Bigfoot vocalizations. Genetic analysis of hair or scat samples, if available, provides the most objective method of species identification. However, interpreting genetic data can be complex, and requires specialized expertise to avoid misleading conclusions. Statistical analysis plays a significant role in evaluating the significance of observed patterns and determining the likelihood of different hypotheses. The application of GIS (Geographic Information Systems) technology helps in mapping potential Bigfoot habitats, identifying areas of high activity, and visualizing potential movement patterns. The goal is to draw objective conclusions based on the available evidence, acknowledging limitations and uncertainties. The interpretation of data should be transparent and replicable, allowing other researchers to scrutinize the findings and contribute to the ongoing investigation. Collaboration and open sharing of data within the scientific community is vital for promoting progress in Bigfoot research. This collaborative approach promotes rigorous peer review, contributing to the enhancement of methodologies and improving the robustness of future investigations. It's a cyclical process; the analysis of existing data informs future investigations, leading to the refinement of tracking, surveillance, and data collection techniques.

The advancement of technology offers ever-evolving tools to further refine investigative methodologies. Remote sensing technologies, such as satellite imagery, can identify potential habitats based on vegetation patterns and terrain characteristics. AI-powered image recognition algorithms are being developed to aid in the identification of potential Bigfoot images or videos within large data sets. Advanced DNA sequencing techniques offer the potential for more precise species identification and potentially phylogenetic analysis, helping to understand Bigfoot's relationship to other primate species. Furthermore, improved understanding of animal behavior and ecology, incorporating insights from related disciplines such as primatology and wildlife biology, provides crucial context for interpreting the field data.

However, the limitations of current investigative techniques are equally important to acknowledge. The elusive nature of the subject significantly complicates the process. The vastness of potential habitats, often located in remote and difficult-to-access regions, limits the scope of investigations. The inherent difficulties of observing and recording a shy, possibly nocturnal creature challenges the reliability of traditional observational methods. Environmental factors, such as weather conditions, also impact data collection and can introduce biases into the results. The possibility of misidentification, whether through human error or the presence of other animals, necessitates a critical and cautious approach to interpreting the collected evidence. The subjective nature of eyewitness accounts, often influenced by preconceived notions and biases, demands careful evaluation and consideration. These limitations underscore the need for rigorous methodology and a critical approach to analysis.

Finally, it is crucial to approach the investigation of Bigfoot with a combination of open-mindedness and robust scientific rigor. While embracing the possibility of the existence of an unknown primate species, a skeptical lens remains essential to ensure that the findings are grounded in verifiable evidence and logical reasoning. The inherent ambiguity of the subject requires embracing uncertainty and acknowledging the limitations of current methodologies. The ongoing investigation is not simply a quest for definitive proof, but a journey of scientific exploration, constantly refining our techniques and pushing the boundaries of our understanding of the natural world. The future of Bigfoot research lies in the continued development and refinement of investigative techniques, along with a collaborative approach that incorporates insights from diverse fields and promotes open communication and data sharing within the scientific community. The quest for Bigfoot, then, is not just about finding a creature, but about pushing the limits of scientific inquiry and enhancing our understanding of the natural world, one footprint, one hair, one piece of scat at a time.

14

CHALLENGES AND ETHICAL
CONSIDERATIONS IN BIGFOOT
RESEARCH

The pursuit of Bigfoot, a creature shrouded in mystery and steeped in folklore, presents researchers with a unique set of challenges. These hurdles aren't simply logistical; they are deeply intertwined with ethical considerations that demand careful navigation. The very nature of the subject – a large, elusive, and potentially endangered primate – necessitates a responsible and ethical approach. The lack of conclusive physical evidence, coupled with the often contradictory eyewitness accounts, adds a layer of complexity. Furthermore, the intense public fascination with Bigfoot often leads to sensationalism and misinformation, making it crucial for researchers to maintain a high degree of scientific rigor and transparency.

One of the most significant challenges lies in the difficulty of verifying evidence. Many purported Bigfoot sightings rely on anecdotal accounts, often colored by personal biases, excitement, or even deliberate deception. Photographs and video footage, while seemingly compelling, are frequently blurry, poorly lit, or easily misinterpreted. Footprints, another common piece of "evidence," are subject to natural processes such as erosion and animal interference, making definitive attribution exceptionally difficult. Even seemingly more concrete evidence like hair samples or scat can be challenging to analyze, requiring advanced techniques and careful consideration of potential contamination or misidentification. The rarity of encounters and the vast, often remote, territories where Bigfoot is allegedly sighted further exacerbate the difficulty of collecting verifiable evidence.

The ethical considerations inherent in Bigfoot research are multifaceted. First and foremost is the potential impact on the environment and any potential Bigfoot population. Intrusive research methods could disturb sensitive ecosystems or inadvertently endanger the creature itself, should it exist. Respect for wilderness areas and minimizing the researcher's ecological footprint are, therefore, critical. Ethical guidelines must prioritize the preservation of habitats and the avoidance of any actions that might harm the environment or any living creatures, known or unknown. This includes strict adherence to regulations regarding wildlife observation and the responsible disposal of any materials used during research expeditions.

Another crucial ethical concern relates to the interaction with the public and the management of expectations. Researchers must strive to avoid fueling misinformation or exploiting the public's interest for personal gain. This means maintaining transparency in research methods, acknowledging the limitations of current evidence, and avoiding sensationalist claims that might mislead or misinform the public. Presenting findings objectively, even if those findings are inconclusive, is vital for maintaining the integrity of the research and fostering trust among the scientific community and the general public. Responsible communication is essential to ensure that the public understands the scientific process and the limitations of the research.

Furthermore, researchers must also be acutely aware of the potential for their work to be misused or misinterpreted. The lack of definitive proof has created an environment where speculative interpretations and unsubstantiated claims can easily gain traction. The challenge is to present the findings in a way that is both scientifically rigorous and accessible to a broader audience without inadvertently feeding into conspiracy theories or generating unwarranted anxieties. The potential for misrepresentation of the research, both deliberate and accidental, emphasizes the need for careful communication and the responsible dissemination of information.

The legal aspects of Bigfoot research also introduce further ethical complexities. Access to private land often requires permission from landowners, and researchers must comply with local laws and regulations regarding wildlife observation and the collection of potential evidence. Furthermore, the legal status of Bigfoot, should it exist, is unclear, raising questions about the legality of its observation, study, or potential interaction. Researchers must meticulously adhere to all relevant laws and regulations and seek proper legal permission where necessary to avoid any legal ramifications.

Another significant ethical challenge revolves around the potential impact on indigenous communities. Bigfoot is deeply rooted in the folklore and traditions of many Native American tribes, who often view the creature with reverence and consider it sacred. Researchers must approach their work with respect for these cultural beliefs and avoid any actions that might be seen as disrespectful or intrusive. Meaningful collaboration with indigenous communities is essential, not only to gain their insights and knowledge but also to demonstrate respect for their traditions and cultural heritage. This includes actively seeking their permission and guidance before undertaking any research that might impact their sacred lands or traditional practices.

The question of research funding also presents ethical dilemmas. The funding sources for Bigfoot research can range from private donations to government grants, and the nature of funding can influence the direction and interpretation of the research. Maintaining independence from outside influences, be they financial or otherwise, is critical for ensuring the objectivity and integrity of the research findings. Transparency regarding funding sources and potential conflicts of interest is essential to build trust and credibility.

Finally, researchers must actively engage in peer review and open communication to ensure the quality and validity of their work. The subjective nature of much Bigfoot evidence necessitates a rigorous review process to avoid biases and promote critical evaluation. Sharing data openly, even if incomplete or inconclusive, fosters collaboration and allows other researchers to verify findings and build upon previous work. This collaborative approach helps to avoid duplication of effort and promotes the overall advancement of Bigfoot research. The scientific method thrives on transparency, critical evaluation, and collaboration, making open communication a fundamental ethical requirement.

In conclusion, Bigfoot research presents a unique intersection of scientific challenges and ethical considerations. The elusive nature of the subject, the lack of definitive evidence, and the intense public interest all necessitate a responsible and rigorous approach. Researchers must carefully consider the environmental impact of their work, manage public expectations responsibly, avoid misrepresentation, and respect the cultural beliefs of indigenous communities. Transparency, collaboration, and a commitment to ethical principles are not only ethically important but also crucial for the credibility and advancement of Bigfoot research. The quest for truth, in this case, demands not only scientific rigor but also a deep sense of responsibility and respect.

15

COLLABORATION AND
COMMUNICATION AMONG
RESEARCHERS

The success of any scientific endeavor hinges not only on individual brilliance but also on the collaborative spirit and effective communication among researchers. Bigfoot research, a field often characterized by its inherent challenges and the controversies surrounding it, is no exception. The lack of concrete physical evidence and the often subjective nature of eyewitness accounts necessitate a robust framework of collaboration and information sharing to effectively sift through the wealth of data and advance the understanding of the subject. Without a systematic approach to collaboration, the field risks becoming fragmented, hindering the progress of scientific inquiry.

Historically, Bigfoot research has suffered from a degree of isolationism amongst researchers. Individual investigators, often driven by passion and personal convictions, have sometimes preferred to hoard their findings, either out of fear of ridicule or a desire to maintain a competitive edge.

This approach has undeniably hampered the field's progress. A single, compelling piece of evidence, however meticulously documented, holds less weight than the accumulation of data from multiple, independent sources. A collaborative approach allows for the cross-checking of information, the identification of biases, and the triangulation of data points to create a more comprehensive and robust picture.

One significant hurdle to effective collaboration is the lack of a centralized, universally accepted database of Bigfoot related information. While several organizations and individuals maintain their own archives, there is no single repository where all relevant data, from eyewitness accounts and photographic evidence to footprint casts and audio recordings, can be accessed and analyzed collectively. The absence of such a repository hampers comparative studies and the identification of patterns that might otherwise be missed. For instance, seemingly disparate accounts from different geographical locations might reveal common threads or consistent behavioral patterns when analyzed together within a centralized database. Such a database, meticulously cataloged and rigorously vetted, would be a significant asset to the field.

The challenge extends beyond simply establishing a database. Effective collaboration requires a standardized methodology for collecting and analyzing data. Different researchers may employ different techniques, leading to inconsistencies and difficulties in comparing results. The standardization of methods, including the way eyewitness testimonies are documented and analyzed, the protocols for collecting physical evidence (such as footprint casts and hair samples), and the guidelines for evaluating photographic or audio evidence, would greatly enhance the credibility and impact of Bigfoot research. This standardization would ensure that data from different sources are comparable and can be integrated into a comprehensive analysis.

Furthermore, the establishment of peer review processes is crucial. The field currently lacks a robust peer-review system akin to that found in established scientific disciplines. The lack of such a system allows for the proliferation of unsubstantiated claims and unreliable data, potentially misleading the public and hindering the credibility of the field. A well-defined peer-review process would subject research findings to scrutiny by experts in relevant fields, ensuring the quality, rigor, and reliability of the research before its publication or dissemination.

Beyond the technical aspects of data collection and analysis, the success of collaborative research depends heavily on effective communication. This necessitates the development of open communication channels between researchers. Regular conferences, workshops, and online forums can serve as platforms for sharing findings, exchanging ideas, and engaging in constructive criticism. These interactions are crucial not only for the advancement of the field but also for fostering a spirit of mutual respect and understanding among researchers. Such open communication can help to bridge divides between researchers with differing methodologies or viewpoints, fostering a more unified approach to the study of Bigfoot.

The potential benefits of enhanced collaboration and communication extend far beyond the immediate goals of Bigfoot research. The insights gained through collaborative efforts can have wider implications for other areas of zoology, primatology, and even conservation biology. Understanding the potential existence of an unknown hominid species could reshape our understanding of human evolution and primate behavior. This information could also inform conservation efforts aimed at protecting unknown species and their habitats.

Another important facet of collaboration in Bigfoot research lies in engaging with local communities, particularly indigenous populations. Many indigenous cultures have long-standing oral traditions and stories related to creatures that bear striking similarities to Bigfoot. These accounts, passed down through generations, represent a valuable source of information that should not be dismissed or underestimated. Collaborating with indigenous communities involves not only gathering information but also engaging in respectful dialogue, acknowledging their knowledge and expertise, and ensuring that their cultural heritage is protected and respected during the research process. This type of collaboration requires a sensitive approach, ensuring that the research process respects cultural sensitivities and avoids exploiting indigenous knowledge for personal gain. It necessitates informed consent, shared benefits, and the recognition of indigenous rights.

The involvement of experts from various disciplines is also crucial. The study of Bigfoot necessitates a multidisciplinary approach, integrating the expertise of zoologists, anthropologists, geneticists, cryptozoologists, and forensic scientists, among others. Each discipline brings a unique perspective and set of skills that can contribute to a more holistic understanding of the subject. For instance, geneticists can analyze DNA samples (if available) to determine the species' lineage and genetic relationships to other known primates. Anthropologists can contribute insights into the behavioral patterns and social structures of Bigfoot, based on interpretations of footprint evidence, anecdotal accounts, and comparisons with known primate societies. Forensic scientists can use their expertise in analyzing physical evidence to verify authenticity and eliminate the possibility of hoaxing or misidentification.

The integration of advanced technologies can significantly enhance collaborative efforts. The use of remote sensing technologies, such as trail cameras, thermal imaging, and acoustic monitoring systems, can greatly expand the scope of data collection. This data can be easily shared and analyzed collectively by researchers across various locations, fostering a collaborative approach. The application of GIS (Geographic Information System) technology is also crucial to map sightings, analyze habitat preferences, and identify potential patterns in Bigfoot activity. Such technological advancements can greatly aid in the standardization of data collection and improve the objectivity and reliability of research findings.

Finally, transparency is paramount. The sharing of data and research findings with the wider scientific community, and indeed the public, is essential for maintaining the integrity and credibility of Bigfoot research. Open access to data allows for independent verification and lets other researchers build upon previous work. While protecting the privacy of individuals and locations may be necessary, ensuring transparency in methods and findings is crucial for fostering trust and building confidence in the research process. The open exchange of information fosters a culture of critical examination and helps to improve the overall quality of research within the field.

In conclusion, the advancement of Bigfoot research depends critically on fostering a culture of collaboration and open communication. The establishment of a centralized database, the standardization of methodologies, the implementation of peer review processes, the engagement with local communities, the incorporation of multidisciplinary expertise, the integration of advanced technologies, and the commitment to transparency are all essential components of a robust and credible research program. Only through a concerted and collaborative effort can we hope to unravel the enduring mystery surrounding this enigmatic creature. The pursuit of truth in this field demands not only rigorous scientific methodology but also a strong commitment to open communication and collaborative scholarship. By embracing these principles, we can hope to move Bigfoot research from the realm of speculation to a more scientifically rigorous and credible pursuit.

16

FUNDING AND SUPPORT FOR BIGFOOT RESEARCH INITIATIVES

The pursuit of Bigfoot, a creature shrouded in mystery and legend, is a costly endeavor. Unlike established scientific fields with robust government and institutional funding, Bigfoot research relies heavily on a patchwork of sources, often reflecting the fringe nature of the subject. This precarious funding landscape directly impacts the scale and scope of investigations, influencing everything from the duration and intensity of fieldwork to the sophistication of the analytical tools employed. Securing consistent and reliable funding remains one of the greatest obstacles to achieving meaningful progress.

Private donations form a significant, though often unpredictable, pillar of support. Numerous organizations dedicated to Bigfoot research rely almost entirely on the generosity of individuals who believe in the cause. These donations, while crucial, frequently come in small amounts, making long-term planning and large-scale projects challenging. Successful fundraising campaigns often rely heavily on the captivating nature of the Bigfoot mystery itself, utilizing compelling imagery and anecdotal evidence to attract contributors. The variability of these donations means that research initiatives can experience periods of plenty and scarcity, impacting the continuity and stability of their operations. Moreover, the reliance on individual donations can create a bias, where research agendas might inadvertently be shaped by the interests of the donors rather than purely scientific objectives.

Grants from private foundations represent another, more stable, source of funding. However, securing these grants is incredibly competitive. Proposals must demonstrate rigorous scientific methodology, clear objectives, and a convincing case for the potential impact of the research. Given the lack of widely accepted physical evidence and the inherent skepticism surrounding Bigfoot research, securing funding from established foundations known for their support of rigorous scientific inquiry can prove incredibly difficult. The review process is often stringent, and proposals may be rejected simply because the subject matter lies outside the conventional scientific paradigm. This competitive landscape necessitates the submission of numerous proposals to maximize the chances of securing funding, adding significant time and resource constraints. Even successful grant applications may only provide partial funding, requiring researchers to continually seek additional resources.

While government funding is rare in Bigfoot research, occasional collaborations or indirect support can occur. For instance, researchers might collaborate with government agencies on projects involving wilderness exploration or wildlife conservation, with Bigfoot research becoming a secondary, albeit related, focus. This indirect support is often limited in scope and duration, making it an unreliable source of consistent funding. The lack of government support further reinforces the perception of Bigfoot research as a less credible scientific pursuit compared to established fields.

Crowdfunding platforms have emerged as a relatively new avenue for securing funds. These platforms allow researchers to directly appeal to a wider audience, bypassing the traditional gatekeepers of scientific funding. While this approach can generate considerable sums, it requires significant outreach efforts and effective communication to attract backers. Transparency and accountability are vital for successful crowdfunding campaigns, requiring researchers to diligently report on the use of funds and to maintain regular communication with their supporters. The success of crowdfunding initiatives often hinges on engaging storytelling and the ability to demonstrate the genuine need for funding and the potential impact of the research.

The Impact of limited and inconsistent funding on Bigfoot research is profound. It directly limits the scale and scope of expeditions, restricting the geographical areas that can be surveyed and the duration of fieldwork. This often translates to less comprehensive data collection and a reduced ability to thoroughly investigate potential leads. Furthermore, the lack of funds can restrict access to cutting-edge technology, such as advanced imaging equipment, DNA analysis tools, and sophisticated data processing capabilities. This technology is vital for identifying and analyzing potential evidence, contributing to a more accurate and reliable understanding of the phenomena.

The financial limitations also affect the ability to recruit and retain qualified researchers. Without adequate funding, researchers often have to rely on personal savings or secondary employment to support their investigations, often leading to burnout and ultimately a reduction in the overall expertise available in the field. The lack of a sustainable career path in Bigfoot research further contributes to this challenge, discouraging younger scientists from pursuing this area of study.

The scarcity of resources also restricts the capacity to engage in crucial activities such as comprehensive data analysis and peer review. Rigorous analysis of data requires skilled personnel and sophisticated software, both of which demand substantial financial investment. The absence of adequate resources often results in limited analysis and a decreased chance of achieving statistically significant results, which in turn affects the credibility and acceptance of the research within the wider scientific community. Similarly, peer review is a cornerstone of scientific integrity, ensuring the validity and reliability of research findings. However, in the case of Bigfoot research, the lack of institutional support often leads to a reduced level of scrutiny and peer-to-peer verification, potentially compromising the overall quality and reliability of the findings.

In conclusion, securing sustainable and adequate funding is paramount to advancing Bigfoot research. The current reliance on unpredictable private donations, challenging grant applications, and the infrequent engagement of government support creates a perpetually unstable funding landscape. This instability directly impacts the scope, scale, quality, and long-term viability of investigations. To enhance the credibility and progress of Bigfoot research, a more diversified and reliable funding model is crucial, demanding a proactive effort to engage private foundations, explore innovative funding mechanisms like crowdfunding, and advocate for increased government support. Only through a commitment to securing stable funding can we hope to rigorously investigate and potentially unravel the enduring mystery of Bigfoot. The financial constraints currently facing researchers are not just a matter of convenience, but a fundamental obstacle to achieving scientific progress in this fascinating and controversial field. The development of a robust, sustainable funding framework is therefore an essential prerequisite for advancing Bigfoot research from a niche area of interest to a scientifically credible and rigorously investigated field. Until this crucial issue is addressed, the persistent mystery of Bigfoot will likely remain shrouded in both legend and financial limitation. The future of Bigfoot research, therefore, hinges not only on scientific ingenuity but also on the pragmatic and successful acquisition of sufficient and reliable financial resources.

17

EXPLAINING SIGHTINGS THROUGH KNOWN ANIMALS

The most straightforward explanation for Bigfoot sightings, and one frequently cited by skeptics, is the misidentification hypothesis. This theory posits that the creatures reported as Bigfoot are actually known animals, often large mammals, observed under conditions that lead to misinterpretation or exaggeration. The vast majority of purported Bigfoot encounters lack high-quality, verifiable evidence, leaving ample room for alternative explanations rooted in known fauna and human perception. This isn't to say that all sightings are definitively misidentifications, but it's a crucial starting point in a rational analysis of the phenomenon.

Several factors contribute to the potential for misidentification. Nocturnal sightings, limited visibility due to weather conditions like fog or heavy rain, and fleeting glimpses at a distance all conspire to hinder accurate identification. Add to this the human tendency towards pareidolia – the perception of familiar patterns in random or ambiguous stimuli – and the likelihood of misidentification increases significantly. We readily see faces in clouds, patterns in wood grain, and even monstrous creatures in the shadows. The psychological predisposition to interpret ambiguous stimuli in a way that confirms pre-existing beliefs – confirmation bias – further complicates the picture. Someone already convinced of Bigfoot's existence might be more likely to interpret a blurry image or unusual sound as evidence supporting their belief, even if a more mundane explanation is plausible.

One common source of misidentification involves bears. Black bears and grizzly bears, particularly when viewed from a distance or in poor light, can appear significantly larger and more imposing than they actually are. Their gait can also be misinterpreted, especially if only glimpses of movement are observed. The size and shape of their footprints, especially in soft or muddy ground, can be distorted, leading to inflated estimations of size. Additionally, bears often exhibit bipedal locomotion, albeit briefly, when standing on their hind legs to reach for food or survey their surroundings. This momentary bipedalism could be easily mistaken for a habitually upright walking creature. Numerous anecdotal reports detail sightings of large, dark, bipedal figures that, upon closer examination of the circumstances and potential alternative explanations, are revealed to be bears exhibiting such behavior.

Similar misidentification scenarios apply to other large mammals found in the environments where Bigfoot sightings are common. Moose, particularly when partially obscured by vegetation or viewed in profile, might be misinterpreted as having a more human-like torso and a less defined neck. Their gait and size can also lead to misjudgments in estimating their dimensions. Elk, deer, and even large dogs under specific lighting conditions and distances could contribute to inaccurate reports. The key here is that these animals, while undeniably distinct from humans in known characteristics, can exhibit certain aspects of their appearance and behavior that, under less-than-ideal observational conditions, could lead to mistaken identification.

Beyond the visual aspects, auditory misinterpretations also play a significant role. The sounds attributed to Bigfoot, often described as loud howls, roars, or strange vocalizations, could originate from a multitude of sources. Animals such as mountain lions, wolves, owls, or even unusual natural phenomena like rockfalls or wind currents through dense forests could create sounds that match the commonly reported descriptions of Bigfoot vocalizations. The lack of high-fidelity recordings and the difficulty in precisely pinpointing the source of the sounds make it difficult to definitively rule out known animals as the origin.

Furthermore, the human tendency to embellish stories, particularly over time, cannot be disregarded. The game of "telephone," where a story is repeatedly retold, resulting in gradual distortion and exaggeration, is a common phenomenon affecting numerous aspects of folklore and storytelling. In the case of Bigfoot, initial encounters that may have involved a relatively commonplace animal could be embellished with each retelling, gradually evolving into tales of a massive, mysterious humanoid creature. The lack of immediate, objective documentation in many instances makes it nearly impossible to disentangle the original event from the subsequent embellishments.

In conclusion, while the misidentification hypothesis does not inherently disprove the existence of Bigfoot, it remains a compelling and often overlooked factor in evaluating the validity of numerous reported sightings. The combination of poor visibility, fleeting glimpses, confirmation bias, the power of suggestion, and the natural tendency for exaggeration renders a considerable proportion of Bigfoot evidence highly susceptible to misinterpretation. A thorough and critical examination of each sighting, focusing on contextual factors and alternative explanations involving known animals, is essential for a rigorous scientific approach to this intriguing phenomenon. Indeed, before assuming the existence of a novel primate, one must thoroughly exhaust all possibilities involving the known. This does not, however, preclude the possibility of additional, yet undiscovered, species inhabiting remote regions, but it does emphasize the importance of skepticism and thorough investigation in evaluating claims of unknown creatures.

Only by carefully considering the potential for misidentification can researchers more reliably focus on anomalous evidence that truly demands a more extraordinary explanation. The challenge lies in separating the wheat from the chaff, the truly anomalous from the easily explained. And that task requires rigorous and open-minded investigation, leaving no stone unturned in the quest for the truth.

18

BIGFOOT AS A CULTURAL PHENOMENON

The possibility that Bigfoot is not a biological entity but rather a purely cultural phenomenon deserves careful consideration. This "folklore hypothesis" suggests that Bigfoot sightings and stories are not rooted in reality but are instead a product of shared cultural narratives, evolving over time and adapting to different contexts. This isn't to dismiss individual accounts as intentional fabrications, but rather to explore the possibility that a deeply ingrained cultural archetype, passed down through generations, might be responsible for the enduring belief in this elusive creature.

Consider the prevalence of large, hairy hominid figures in folklore across diverse cultures worldwide. From the Yeti of the Himalayas to the Yeren of China, and the various wild men and woodwoses of European mythology, the basic narrative structure remains remarkably consistent: a large, bipedal, hairy creature inhabiting remote wilderness areas. These stories often function as cautionary tales, warnings to stay within the bounds of civilization, or serve as explanations for unexplained natural phenomena. The common threads in these narratives suggest a deeply ingrained human tendency to populate the unknown with mythical figures, reflecting our anxieties and fascination with the untamed wilderness.

The very act of reporting a Bigfoot sighting might be influenced by these pre-existing narratives. Individuals encountering unusual sounds or tracks in the woods may unconsciously interpret these ambiguous stimuli through the lens of established Bigfoot lore. The power of suggestion is potent; once the idea of Bigfoot is introduced, it can influence perception and interpretation of ambiguous evidence. This is further compounded by confirmation bias, a cognitive bias that leads individuals to seek out and interpret information that confirms their pre-existing beliefs, while dismissing contradictory evidence. A hiker who believes in Bigfoot, upon encountering a large footprint, might be more inclined to interpret it as evidence of the creature than someone who is skeptical.

The evolution of the Bigfoot narrative itself is also compelling evidence for the folklore hypothesis. Early accounts of Bigfoot often differ significantly from modern descriptions. In some cases, the creature is described as almost monstrous, possessing aggressive tendencies and a propensity for violence. In others, it is portrayed as more reclusive and enigmatic, avoiding human contact. These variations suggest an evolving myth, adapting to changing cultural contexts and perceptions. The media's role in shaping public perception is undeniable. The sensationalization of Bigfoot sightings and the proliferation of blurry photographs and grainy videos have only served to amplify and perpetuate the myth.

Furthermore, the geographical distribution of Bigfoot sightings correlates strikingly with areas rich in established folklore concerning similar creatures. The concentration of reports in the Pacific Northwest of North America, for instance, coincides with a region with a long and vibrant history of indigenous legends featuring large, hairy hominids. This correlation strengthens the hypothesis that the belief in Bigfoot might be a geographically rooted cultural phenomenon rather than a reflection of an actual biological entity.

The persistence of the Bigfoot belief in the face of a lack of conclusive scientific evidence further supports the folklore hypothesis. Despite decades of dedicated research, no definitive proof of

Bigfoot's existence has been found. The absence of conclusive physical evidence, such as skeletal remains, clear high-quality photographs, or DNA samples, casts significant doubt on the biological reality of Bigfoot. If a creature as large and allegedly widespread as Bigfoot truly existed, one would expect to find more readily verifiable evidence.

The enduring power of folklore should not be underestimated. Stories and legends, transmitted orally across generations, possess a remarkable ability to shape collective beliefs and perceptions. The transmission of these stories through oral tradition, coupled with the amplification effect of modern media, could readily explain the widespread and enduring belief in Bigfoot without requiring the existence of a novel primate species.

The psychological aspects of belief are also critical. The human desire to believe in the mysterious, the unknown, and the possibility of something extraordinary is a powerful force. Bigfoot, as a symbolic representation of the untamed wilderness and the unknown, taps into this fundamental human desire. The thrill of the hunt, the mystery surrounding the creature, and the potential for a groundbreaking discovery all contribute to the appeal of the Bigfoot enigma.

The debate around Bigfoot isn't merely a scientific inquiry; it's a reflection of broader cultural trends and psychological predispositions. The allure of Bigfoot extends far beyond simple misidentification; it represents our fascination with mystery, our desire to believe in something extraordinary, and our deep-seated connection to the wilderness and its inherent unknowability.

The enduring nature of Bigfoot stories, despite the lack of definitive proof, highlights the powerful role of cultural narratives in shaping human beliefs. The consistency of the descriptions across cultures and time periods, the correlation between sighting locations and established folklore traditions, and the psychological appeal of the Bigfoot myth all contribute to the plausibility of the folklore hypothesis.

It is important to note that the folklore hypothesis doesn't necessarily exclude the possibility of other explanations, such as misidentification or even the existence of an undiscovered primate. Rather, it presents a compelling alternative explanation, one that acknowledges the potent influence of cultural narratives and human psychology in shaping our understanding of the natural world and the unknown.

It is also crucial to approach this analysis with a level of respectful awareness of indigenous cultures and their traditions. Many indigenous communities possess longstanding oral histories and deeply held beliefs about creatures inhabiting the wilderness. Dismissing these traditions as mere folklore risks overlooking valuable cultural knowledge and potentially causing offense. Instead, a nuanced understanding that incorporates both scientific skepticism and respectful consideration of cultural perspectives is essential.

Ultimately, the question of Bigfoot's existence remains open. While the possibility of a previously unknown primate species cannot be completely ruled out, the compelling evidence presented by the folklore hypothesis warrants serious consideration. The persistent sightings, the lack of definitive proof, and the rich tapestry of related folklore worldwide suggest that the Bigfoot phenomenon may be far more complex than a simple case of misidentification. It could be a powerful illustration of the enduring power of cultural narratives to shape human beliefs and perceptions of the world around us, reminding us of the importance of critical thinking, careful analysis, and a respectful approach to the diverse interpretations of the natural world. The debate, therefore, extends beyond the realm of zoology and touches upon the broader fields of anthropology, cultural studies, and psychology, enriching our understanding of human nature and the enduring power of myth. The mystery of Bigfoot, whatever its ultimate explanation, continues to fuel our imaginations and provoke crucial questions about how we perceive and interact with the unknown. The search for Bigfoot, consequently, is as much a search for understanding human belief systems as it is a quest for a particular creature.

19

SCIENTIFIC ARGUMENTS FOR A NEW PRIMATE

T he enduring mystery of Bigfoot compels us to consider a more scientifically grounded explanation: the undiscovered species hypothesis. This theory posits that Bigfoot is, in fact, a previously unknown hominid species, a large, bipedal primate that has somehow eluded scientific discovery until now. While seemingly extraordinary, this hypothesis holds merit when considering the vast unexplored regions of the world, particularly dense forested areas with limited human access. The Amazon rainforest, the Congo Basin, and remote parts of Southeast Asia, for example, are still relatively uncharted territories, harboring potential for undiscovered species of all kinds. The sheer scale of these wildernesses makes it plausible that a large, elusive creature like Bigfoot could have remained undetected for centuries.

The argument for an undiscovered primate gains traction when we consider the historical record of primate discovery. Throughout the 20th century alone, several new primate species were identified, demonstrating that our understanding of primate biodiversity is constantly evolving. The discovery of the bonobo in the 1930s, for example, highlighted the potential for entirely new primate species to be found, even in areas that had been previously explored to some extent. Similarly, discoveries of new species in relatively well-studied regions like Madagascar emphasize the limitations of our current knowledge. Given the remote and challenging terrain typically associated with Bigfoot sightings, the possibility that a large, intelligent primate remains undiscovered should not be readily dismissed.

Furthermore, anecdotal evidence cited by Bigfoot researchers often includes descriptions of physical characteristics that differ significantly from known primate species. Accounts frequently describe creatures of exceptional size and stature, with an unusual gait and body proportions. While photographic and video evidence has often been disputed due to poor quality or potential hoaxes, some proponents claim to show distinctive physical features, such as unusually large feet and a pronounced musculature, that do not readily align with any known species. The interpretation of this evidence remains highly debated, however the sheer volume of these accounts across various geographical locations and time periods warrants consideration, even if individually the evidence may be insufficient.

The challenge lies in reconciling these anecdotal accounts with the scarcity of definitive physical proof. The lack of complete skeletal remains, irrefutable DNA samples, or clear high-resolution photographic evidence continues to fuel skepticism. Critics rightly point out that the absence of such irrefutable evidence significantly weakens the undiscovered species hypothesis. Many argue that the accumulated evidence, even when considered collectively, is too circumstantial to support the claim of a new hominid species. It is crucial to acknowledge this skepticism and to examine the potential for alternative explanations, such as misidentification of known animals, deliberate hoaxes, or even psychological factors influencing eyewitness accounts.

However, the limitations of current research methods also need to be considered. Traditional methods of wildlife research, often based on direct observation and trapping, are largely ineffective when dealing with a creature as elusive and intelligent as Bigfoot is purported to be. The creature's apparent ability to avoid detection, coupled with its presumed intelligence and cautious behavior, significantly hinders the application of standard scientific methodologies.

This makes it challenging for scientists to gather the conclusive evidence required to prove the existence of a new primate species using traditional approaches. The reliance on often-subjective eyewitness accounts, blurry photographs, and ambiguous footprint casts makes the task even more difficult.

The development of new technologies, however, presents new opportunities for advancing Bigfoot research. Advanced DNA analysis techniques, for example, offer the potential to identify previously unknown species from minute environmental samples, such as hair, feces, or saliva. Camera trap technology, using motion-activated cameras strategically placed in suspected Bigfoot habitats, may also provide more conclusive visual evidence than anecdotal accounts can offer. Similarly, the use of advanced acoustic monitoring equipment can help identify unique vocalizations or other sounds that might aid in locating and studying the creature. The application of these technologies, coupled with a more sophisticated understanding of the creature's likely habitat and behavior, could significantly enhance the potential for confirming or refuting the undiscovered species hypothesis.

The geographical distribution of Bigfoot sightings also warrants closer examination. While many reports originate from remote and forested regions of North America, similar reports from other parts of the world, such as the Himalayas and the forests of Southeast Asia, suggest the possibility of a wider distribution than currently recognized. The consistent description of a large, bipedal, hairy creature across these vastly different regions raises intriguing questions about the potential for a broader, undiscovered hominid lineage. A thorough comparative analysis of anecdotal accounts and physical evidence from various geographical locations may reveal previously unrecognized patterns, potentially hinting at a wider distribution and greater diversity than is suggested by the concentration of sightings in North America.

Furthermore, understanding the ecology and behavior of Bigfoot, as it's described, is crucial to assessing the validity of the undiscovered species hypothesis. The apparent ability of this hypothetical creature to remain undetected for so long suggests a remarkable capacity for evasiveness and camouflage. This raises the question of its dietary habits, social structure, and interactions with its environment. If Bigfoot indeed exists, understanding its ecological niche and behavioral strategies would be essential in developing effective research methods for its detection and study. Researchers would need to develop strategies to locate the creature by understanding its preferred habitats, feeding patterns, and the impact it might have on the surrounding ecosystem.

The possibility of a new primate species coexisting with humans, undetected for so long, necessitates a re-evaluation of our understanding of primate evolution and biodiversity. The discovery of such a creature would have profound implications for our understanding of human origins and the evolutionary history of primates, potentially challenging existing evolutionary models and shedding new light on the processes that have shaped primate diversity. The sheer implications of such a discovery go beyond the realm of cryptozoology and touch upon the very core of biological sciences.

However, it's equally important to acknowledge the limitations and potential biases of the data currently available. Much of the evidence presented in support of the undiscovered species hypothesis is anecdotal and open to alternative interpretations. This makes it vital for researchers to maintain a critical and skeptical approach, carefully evaluating the credibility of eyewitness accounts and rigorously testing the validity of all purported evidence. The scientific method requires rigorous scrutiny and a cautious approach to avoid drawing premature conclusions. It's important to acknowledge the possibility of misidentification, hoaxing, or the influence of psychological factors on eyewitness testimony, and these factors must be considered in any evaluation of the evidence.

In conclusion, the undiscovered species hypothesis offers a scientifically plausible, yet challenging, explanation for the Bigfoot phenomenon. While the lack of definitive physical evidence continues to fuel skepticism, the sheer volume of eyewitness accounts, the intriguing descriptions of physical characteristics, and the potential for applying new technologies to the investigation warrant a continued, thorough, and rigorous examination of this hypothesis. The possibility that an undiscovered primate species exists, thriving undetected in the world's remote wildernesses, remains an exciting – and scientifically significant – proposition. Further research, utilizing advanced methodologies and a critical assessment of all available data, will be essential in either confirming or refuting this intriguing and long-standing mystery.

20

A LINK TO OUR ANCESTORS

The undiscovered species hypothesis, while compelling, leaves unanswered questions regarding the creature's longevity and evolutionary path. Could Bigfoot represent not a newly discovered species, but a surviving remnant of an extinct hominid lineage? This "extinct hominid hypothesis" proposes that Bigfoot is a surviving population of a species previously believed to have vanished from the fossil record. This isn't a new idea; it taps into long-standing debates surrounding the gaps in our understanding of human evolution. The fossil record, while constantly expanding, remains incomplete, and many branches of the hominid family tree remain poorly understood, or even entirely unknown.

The discovery of *Homo floresiensis* , nicknamed "Hobbit," on the Indonesian island of Flores in 2003, serves as a powerful example. This diminutive hominin, standing just over three feet tall, defied expectations and highlighted the potential for unexpected hominin diversity. Its existence demonstrated that hominins could thrive in isolated environments, evolving along unique evolutionary trajectories, separate from the lineage leading to modern humans. The "Hobbit" illustrates that even relatively recently, hominid species we previously considered extinct might have persisted in isolated pockets of the world, unknown to science until a remarkable discovery.

Applying this principle to Bigfoot necessitates considering various extinct hominin species. Could Bigfoot be a descendant of *Gigantopithecus* , a massive ape known from fossil teeth and jawbones found in Asia? While *Gigantopithecus* fossils suggest a creature of immense size, it's crucial to emphasize that these fossils are limited, providing only a partial picture. The exact anatomy, locomotion, and even social structure of *Gigantopithecus* remain largely mysterious, leaving open the possibility that it may have possessed characteristics that align with Bigfoot descriptions. The sheer size of *Gigantopithecus*, exceding even the largest gorillas, certainly offers a tempting connection to the reported size of Bigfoot. However, it's important to note that the available fossil evidence is insufficient to definitively confirm or refute a connection. The dating of *Gigantopithecus* fossils places them in a timeframe that allows for the theoretical possibility of surviving populations, particularly if those populations occupied isolated and protected habitats.

Another extinct hominin that has fueled speculation is *Homo erectus*. This species exhibited a relatively modern body plan, suggesting bipedal locomotion, and possessed a larger brain capacity than earlier hominins. *Homo erectus* had a significantly wider geographic distribution than many other hominins, further enhancing the plausibility that isolated populations might have survived undetected. However, the skeletal morphology of *Homo erectus* is notably different from the commonly reported descriptions of Bigfoot, creating a substantial challenge for this hypothesis. The descriptions of Bigfoot often point towards a more robust and heavily muscled build than is evident in the *Homo erectus* fossil record. Nevertheless, the possibility that an isolated population of *Homo erectus* may have exhibited variations or adaptations unavailable for study cannot be entirely discounted.

The limitations of the fossil record must continually be emphasized. Fossilisation is a rare and unpredictable process. Certain environments are more conducive to fossil preservation than others, leading to inevitable biases in our understanding of past life forms. The possibility that substantial hominin populations lived and died without leaving readily discoverable fossil remains cannot be ignored. Dense, humid environments, which would also happen to be ideal habitats for creatures like Bigfoot, are less likely to yield well-preserved fossils.

Furthermore, the sheer expanse of unexplored wilderness on Earth, especially in regions with rugged terrain and dense vegetation, presents a significant challenge to traditional paleontological approaches. Even with modern technology, locating and excavating fossils in such areas can be extremely difficult, labor-intensive, and expensive. The remoteness of many locations cited for Bigfoot sightings further supports the plausibility that undiscovered fossils, or even existing populations of extinct hominids, could be present.

This approach, however, shouldn't discount the role of genetic evidence. While the acquisition of Bigfoot DNA remains elusive, advances in ancient DNA extraction and analysis are continuously improving. Hypothetically, finding genetic material from purported Bigfoot remains could be compared to the genomes of known extinct hominins, potentially revealing evolutionary relationships. Although the possibility of contamination and the challenges in obtaining authentic samples present formidable hurdles, the potential benefits of this approach are undeniable. If a verifiable genetic link could be established between Bigfoot and an extinct hominin species, this would represent a profound discovery, revolutionizing our understanding of human evolution and the biodiversity of our planet.

However, the lack of conclusive physical evidence remains a significant obstacle. While eyewitness accounts and alleged footprints abound, these lack the scientific rigor necessary to definitively prove the existence of a previously unknown hominin. Footprints, particularly, are notoriously difficult to definitively attribute to a specific species due to the variability caused by terrain, weight, and even the angle of the print. Further complicating matters, many purported Bigfoot sightings can be explained by misidentification of known animals, such as bears or other primates.

Ultimately, the extinct hominid hypothesis for Bigfoot's existence presents a fascinating and thought-provoking scenario. It combines our understanding of human evolution with the persistent enigma of Bigfoot. While currently speculative, the hypothesis remains a valid area of investigation. Further research, incorporating cutting-edge technology and rigorous scientific methods, coupled with a renewed focus on examining the limitations of current paleontological knowledge, could provide answers. Until then, the mystery endures, inviting continued scrutiny and fostering a blend of scientific inquiry and the enduring allure of the unknown. The possibility that a surviving lineage of an extinct hominin species roams the Earth today holds a potent appeal to our imagination and drives the persistent investigation into this compelling mystery. The scientific endeavor to understand Bigfoot is not just about discovering a new species; it's about deepening our understanding of the complex tapestry of life on our planet, potentially revising established theories of human evolution, and acknowledging the vast, largely unexplored wilderness still holding secrets that remain hidden from our current knowledge. The future of Bigfoot research, therefore, lies not just in finding concrete evidence but also in refining methodologies, embracing new technologies, and continuing to challenge previously held assumptions about hominin evolution and distribution.

21

STRENGTHS AND WEAKNESSES

The preceding discussion of the extinct hominid hypothesis leaves us with a crucial next step: a thorough evaluation of the evidence supporting each theory of Bigfoot's existence. This involves not only assessing the positive evidence—the eyewitness accounts, purported footprints, and blurry photographs—but also critically examining the limitations and potential flaws in each line of reasoning. Let's proceed with a comparative analysis, acknowledging the inherent challenges in evaluating such elusive and often circumstantial evidence.

The "undiscovered species" hypothesis, while intuitively appealing, faces significant hurdles. Its primary strength lies in the sheer vastness of unexplored wilderness areas globally. The Amazon rainforest, remote regions of Siberia, and the dense forests of North America all provide ample habitat for a large, elusive creature to remain undetected. This possibility is bolstered by the continued discovery of new species, even relatively large animals, in these remote locations, demonstrating that our understanding of biodiversity is far from complete. However, the weaknesses are substantial. The lack of conclusive physical evidence—a complete skeleton, verifiable DNA, or high-quality photographic or video documentation—

casts a long shadow over this theory. While anecdotal evidence abounds, the inherent subjectivity and potential for misidentification, deliberate hoaxing, or even simple misinterpretations severely undermine the reliability of eyewitness accounts. The absence of any consistent morphological characteristics across purported Bigfoot sightings also weakens this hypothesis. Variations in reported size, coloration, and physical features suggest the possibility of multiple unrelated phenomena being conflated under the single label of "Bigfoot."

Furthermore, the sheer longevity attributed to the hypothetical undiscovered species poses a considerable challenge. Maintaining a viable, reproductively successful population of large mammals undetected for an extended period, possibly millennia, strains the bounds of believability. Ecological considerations also come into play. The significant ecological footprint a large, apex predator population would leave behind—changes in prey populations, disruption of established ecosystems, etc.— would be extremely difficult to reconcile with the lack of demonstrable ecological impact associated with Bigfoot. Therefore, while the possibility of an undiscovered species cannot be entirely dismissed, the absence of robust, verifiable evidence heavily weighs against this theory.

The "extinct hominid" hypothesis, while equally speculative, presents a different set of strengths and weaknesses. Its strength lies in its potential to explain some of the observed characteristics attributed to Bigfoot, particularly the apparent bipedal locomotion and purportedly large size. The discovery of new hominin fossils continues to reshape our understanding of human evolution, continually revealing a more complex and diverse picture than previously assumed. The gaps in the fossil record, and the potential for undiscovered hominin lineages, provide a plausible, albeit theoretical, framework for the existence of a surviving population of an extinct hominin species. However, this hypothesis is hampered by the same lack of conclusive physical evidence as the undiscovered species theory. The absence of any verifiable fossil remains attributable to a Bigfoot-like creature, even fragmented ones, seriously undermines this explanation. Furthermore, the sheer time scale involved presents a significant challenge. Extinct hominin species typically disappeared due to environmental changes, competition for resources, or disease, all of which should have significant impacts on the survivability of a small, isolated population over extended periods. Moreover, the genetic implications remain a significant hurdle. If Bigfoot is a surviving hominin, what is its genetic relationship to other known hominin species? Where are the transitional fossil forms that would be expected to bridge the gap between known extinct hominins and Bigfoot? The complete lack of such fossil evidence significantly weakens this theory.

Another prevalent theory, often cited as a counter explanation to Bigfoot sightings, attributes the phenomena to misidentification of known animals. Bears, particularly in poor visibility or under stress, can exhibit behaviors and appearances that might be misinterpreted as those of a large, bipedal creature. Similarly, large primates like gorillas (were they present in the appropriate habitat) or even large, unusual canids could be responsible for some of the reported sightings. This explanation's strength lies in its parsimony — it relies on known entities and does not necessitate the existence of an unknown creature. It also explains away many of the questionable eyewitness testimonies and blurry photographic evidence. However, this theory falls short in explaining the consistency of reported sightings across vast geographical areas and the persistence of the belief in Bigfoot across many diverse cultures and centuries. While misidentification undoubtedly plays a role in some reported sightings, it's unlikely to account for the sheer volume and persistence of Bigfoot-related reports. The numerous accounts that describe features inconsistent with any known animal suggest something more complex is at play.

The "hoax" hypothesis, while seemingly simple, presents significant complexities. Deliberate attempts to fabricate evidence, from staged photographs and planted footprints to elaborate hoaxes involving costumes and sound effects, are documented and undoubtedly contribute to the overall Bigfoot narrative. The strength of this hypothesis lies in its ability to explain away some instances of purported evidence. However, the sheer number and spread of Bigfoot sightings, coupled with accounts from independent and seemingly credible sources, makes the proposition that all these incidents are elaborate and coordinated hoaxes incredibly implausible. The possibility of isolated hoaxes or individual instances of deception cannot be ruled out, but it's improbable to account for the persistence and breadth of Bigfoot mythology across cultures and geographic regions as an outcome of widespread and coordinated deception.

Finally, the possibility of a psychological or collective belief system also demands consideration. The "cultural myth" hypothesis suggests that Bigfoot represents a manifestation of collective unconscious desires, fears, or anxieties projected onto the natural world. Anthropological evidence suggests that many cultures, particularly those with strong ties to nature, have stories and beliefs concerning large, mysterious creatures inhabiting the wilderness. This theory's strength lies in its ability to explain the enduring nature of the Bigfoot myth, its presence across diverse cultures, and its resilience in the face of seemingly disconfirming evidence. It acknowledges the psychological power of stories and their role in shaping our perceptions and understanding of the world. However, its weakness lies in its inability to explain reported physical evidence. While it addresses the persistence of the belief system, it cannot account for the reported physical traces like footprints, hair samples, and vocalizations that some researchers attribute to Bigfoot.

In conclusion, a comprehensive evaluation of the evidence reveals that each theory concerning Bigfoot's existence has its strengths and weaknesses. None definitively proves or disproves the creature's existence. The lack of conclusive physical evidence presents a significant hurdle for all theories requiring the existence of a novel species or surviving hominin population. However, the persistence of reports, the consistency of certain features across accounts, and the enduring cultural resonance of Bigfoot create a complex enigma that resists straightforward explanation. The challenge for future research is not necessarily to find a definitive answer, but to improve methodologies for evidence gathering and analysis, to employ advanced technologies for detection and identification, and to develop a more nuanced understanding of the interplay between observation, belief, and the extraordinary complexities of the natural world. Ultimately, the mystery of Bigfoot serves as a powerful reminder of the vast unknowns that remain, and the importance of maintaining critical thought and rigorous scientific inquiry in the pursuit of understanding our planet and its inhabitants. The investigation continues.

22

COGNITIVE BIASES AND THE INTERPRETATION OF AMBIGUOUS EVIDENCE

The search for Sasquatch, a creature shrouded in mystery and surrounded by conflicting accounts, is fertile ground for the examination of cognitive biases. The very nature of the evidence – often blurry photographs, indistinct footprints, and anecdotal accounts – lends itself to subjective interpretation, heavily influenced by pre-existing beliefs and expectations. This makes understanding the psychological factors at play crucial in evaluating the credibility of claims. One of the most significant biases is confirmation bias, a well-documented tendency to favor information confirming pre-existing beliefs while dismissing or downplaying contradictory evidence. Those who already believe in Sasquatch tend to interpret ambiguous data as supporting evidence, while skeptics dismiss the same data as inconclusive or fabricated.

For instance, a blurry image might be viewed by a believer as a partially obscured Sasquatch, while a skeptic might attribute it to a misidentified animal or a deliberate hoax. Similarly, a large footprint might be interpreted by a believer as definitive proof, while a skeptic might point to the lack of clear contextual evidence, such as clear tracks leading to and from the print, or any other corroborating evidence. The subjective nature of interpretation is further exacerbated by the lack of controlled scientific data. Unlike established scientific fields, Bigfoot research lacks the rigorous methodology and controlled experiments necessary to eliminate subjectivity and minimize bias. This absence of controlled settings leaves the interpretation of evidence open to significant influence by individual biases.

Another influential bias is the availability heuristic, which involves overestimating the likelihood of events that are easily recalled or vividly remembered. Numerous books, documentaries, and anecdotal accounts of Sasquatch sightings contribute to the widespread availability of such narratives. This heightened availability, irrespective of the actual frequency of verified sightings, can lead individuals to overestimate the probability of Sasquatch's existence. Conversely, the lack of definitive scientific proof might lead skeptics to underestimate the possibility, despite the persistence of anecdotal accounts and blurry images. The power of storytelling also plays a critical role. Compelling narratives about Bigfoot encounters, even if lacking rigorous scientific evidence, can sway opinions, particularly when presented with vivid descriptions and emotional appeals.

The Impact of eyewitness testimony in Bigfoot investigations highlights the influence of cognitive biases. Eyewitnesses are often prone to memory distortions, influenced by factors such as stress, fear, and the passage of time. Furthermore, the cultural context of the witness plays a significant role. Individuals familiar with Bigfoot folklore might be more inclined to interpret ambiguous stimuli as consistent with Sasquatch, while those unfamiliar with the legend might offer alternative explanations. This highlights the importance of critically evaluating eyewitness accounts, considering their potential for bias and acknowledging the limitations of human memory. The phenomenon of pareidolia, the tendency to perceive meaningful patterns in random or ambiguous stimuli, further complicates the interpretation of evidence. Shapes in the woods, unusual sounds, and indistinct forms in photographs can be interpreted as Sasquatch by those predisposed to believe, while skeptics would attribute them to natural phenomena or misinterpretations. This perceptual bias is deeply ingrained in human cognition and makes objective evaluation difficult.

The notorious Patterson-Gimlin film, perhaps the most famous piece of purported Bigfoot evidence, is a prime example of how cognitive biases shape interpretation. Believers point to the creature's apparent gait and size as supporting evidence, while skeptics emphasize the film's low quality, lack of detailed corroborating information, and the possibility of a hoax. This divergence of interpretation is largely due to pre-existing beliefs and the selective use of evidence that confirms those beliefs. Furthermore, the lack of clarity in the footage allows for numerous interpretations, each consistent with the viewer's prior expectations.

The role of groupthink In shaping beliefs about Sasquatch Is also significant. Within communities of believers, there's a tendency towards conformity, where dissenting opinions are suppressed or marginalized. This reinforces pre-existing beliefs and creates an echo chamber where confirmation bias is amplified. This group dynamic can further limit objective evaluation and hinder the critical assessment of evidence. Conversely, skepticism can also manifest as a form of groupthink, where skeptical communities reject any evidence that contradicts their preconceived notions, fostering a similar bias towards the dismissal of ambiguous information.

The psychology of deception and hoaxes adds another layer of complexity to the Bigfoot enigma. The deliberate fabrication of evidence, whether for financial gain or personal notoriety, can profoundly influence public perception. The motivation behind such hoaxes, often involving a desire for attention or financial reward, can exploit cognitive biases, making it difficult to distinguish genuine evidence from fabricated claims. Understanding the psychological motivations behind deception is critical in evaluating the credibility of Bigfoot evidence.

To navigate the complexities of Sasquatch research, it is essential to approach the subject with a balanced perspective, acknowledging the potential influence of cognitive biases. This requires a rigorous approach to evidence evaluation, a willingness to consider alternative explanations, and an understanding of the psychological factors that can shape interpretation. By acknowledging the potential for bias in both belief and skepticism, researchers and the public alike can engage with the evidence more critically and objectively, facilitating a more nuanced understanding of the Bigfoot phenomenon. The ambiguity inherent in the evidence surrounding Sasquatch necessitates a cautious approach to interpretation, fostering a healthy skepticism while remaining open to the possibility of previously unknown phenomena. Ultimately, a truly scientific approach must prioritize rigorous methodologies, controlled experiments, and objective data analysis, acknowledging the limitations of subjective interpretation and the pervasive influence of cognitive biases. Only through this critical lens can we approach the mysteries surrounding Sasquatch with the necessary intellectual honesty and integrity. The enduring mystery of Sasquatch lies not only in the elusive nature of the creature itself, but also in the complex interplay of human perception, belief, and the biases that shape our understanding of the world around us. The challenge, therefore, is to disentangle these intertwined factors to arrive at a more reasoned and informed assessment of the evidence.

23

CONFIRMATION BIAS AND THE SEARCH FOR SUPPORTING EVIDENCE

Confirmation bias, the tendency to search for, interpret, favor, and recall information in a way that confirms or supports one's prior beliefs or values, is a potent force in the Bigfoot debate. It's a cognitive shortcut, a mental heuristic that streamlines processing vast amounts of information. In the case of Bigfoot, this means that believers often selectively focus on evidence that supports the creature's existence, while overlooking or discounting contradictory evidence. A blurry photograph, for instance, might be interpreted as undeniable proof by a believer, emphasizing the suggestive aspects of the image and dismissing the lack of clarity as a result of poor lighting or distance. A skeptic, however, might immediately highlight the lack of detail, focusing on the ambiguity and suggesting a misidentification or hoax. The same piece of evidence, then, is filtered through the lens of pre-existing belief, leading to radically different interpretations.

This isn't to say that believers are inherently dishonest or deliberately misleading. Confirmation bias is an unconscious process; it operates subtly and often outside of conscious awareness. It's a fundamental aspect of human cognition, affecting everyone, regardless of their position on Bigfoot. The difference lies in the degree to which individuals are aware of their biases and make efforts to mitigate their influence. The challenge in the Bigfoot research lies in the inherent ambiguity of much of the evidence. Footprints, hair samples, and eyewitness accounts are all subject to various interpretations, and the lack of high-quality, irrefutable evidence leaves room for confirmation bias to flourish.

Consider the frequent reports of "Bigfoot" sightings in remote, wooded areas. Believers might interpret these reports as consistent with the creature's elusive nature and preference for habitats undisturbed by human activity. They might point to the difficulty of tracking and observing large animals in dense forests as evidence of Bigfoot's skillful evasion. Skeptics, on the other hand, might focus on the lack of conclusive physical evidence accompanying these sightings, highlighting the possibility of misidentification of other animals (bears, for instance, or even unusual human activity), and noting the significant influence of storytelling and exaggeration in oral accounts passed down through generations. Both are using the same basic evidence – eyewitness testimony from remote locations – but arriving at dramatically opposite conclusions, demonstrating the power of confirmation bias.

Further exacerbating the problem is the lack of standardized methodologies in Bigfoot research. While some researchers employ rigorous scientific methods, others rely heavily on anecdotal evidence and subjective interpretations. This lack of consistency creates an uneven playing field, making it difficult to assess the credibility of different claims. A poorly conducted investigation, prone to methodological flaws, can generate "evidence" that easily lends itself to confirmation bias. Conversely, rigorous scientific studies which fail to find evidence of Bigfoot are often dismissed by believers as flawed or insufficient, reinforcing their pre-existing beliefs and providing further justification for their pre-conceived notions.

The internet has only intensified the impact of confirmation bias. Online forums and social media platforms allow believers to share and reinforce their interpretations of evidence, creating echo chambers where dissenting opinions are often marginalized or attacked. This self-reinforcing cycle further solidifies pre-existing beliefs, making it increasingly challenging to engage in objective and rational discussion. The proliferation of manipulated images and videos, often presented as proof of Bigfoot's existence, further fuels this cycle. While some deliberate hoaxes exist, many examples represent a complex interplay of wishful thinking and confirmation bias on the part of those who create and share them. They inadvertently—or deliberately —provide further "evidence" for those already inclined to believe.

One of the most striking examples of confirmation bias in Bigfoot research involves the analysis of purported Bigfoot footprints. Large, unusual prints found in muddy areas have been cited as incontrovertible evidence. However, these prints are often subject to multiple interpretations. Believers may emphasize the size and unusual characteristics of the prints, suggesting the tracks are far too large to be from any known animal. Skeptics, on the other hand, might point to the lack of consistent features across different prints and the possibility of hoaxing, manipulation, or misidentification of natural formations. They may also emphasize the lack of corroborating evidence, such as clear video footage or further physical samples linked to the footprint discovery. This same dynamic plays out with purported Bigfoot hair samples, vocalizations, and even eyewitness accounts.

The challenge lies not in eliminating confirmation bias entirely— a virtually impossible task—but in acknowledging its presence and mitigating its influence. This requires a conscious effort to actively seek out and evaluate contradictory evidence, to critically examine the methodologies used in research, and to remain open to alternative explanations. It means approaching the evidence with a healthy skepticism, constantly questioning assumptions and challenging interpretations. This also demands a high level of critical thinking skills, requiring researchers and enthusiasts alike to separate valid evidence from anecdotal claims, and reliably distinguish between objective data and subjective interpretations.

Furthermore, the development and application of rigorous, standardized research methodologies are crucial. This would involve implementing consistent protocols for data collection, analysis, and interpretation, reducing the subjective element in Bigfoot research. Such standardized protocols would also incorporate techniques to address and minimize potential biases during the data collection and analysis phases of the research process. For instance, blinding procedures could be implemented, where researchers are unaware of the source or potential significance of the samples they are analyzing, minimizing the influence of pre-existing beliefs. This would ensure greater transparency and improve the reliability of the resulting data.

The use of advanced technological tools, such as DNA analysis, thermal imaging, and remote sensing technologies, can also significantly contribute to a more objective and reliable assessment of the evidence. While these tools do not guarantee conclusive proof of Bigfoot's existence, they can help to reduce the influence of subjective interpretations and potentially reveal new information that would otherwise remain hidden. However, even advanced technology cannot fully negate the possibility of misinterpretations or errors. Therefore, a critical and rigorous approach to data interpretation remains essential.

In conclusion, the search for Bigfoot is a fascinating case study in the psychology of belief and skepticism. The ambiguous nature of the evidence, coupled with the powerful influence of confirmation bias, creates a complex and challenging landscape for researchers. Overcoming the influence of confirmation bias requires a conscious effort to approach the evidence with open-mindedness, a critical eye, and a willingness to consider alternative explanations, acknowledging the inherent limitations of human perception and the enduring power of pre-existing beliefs. The pursuit of truth and understanding concerning the Bigfoot phenomenon ultimately hinges on developing and implementing rigorous methodologies, utilizing advanced technology responsibly, and acknowledging the ever-present role of cognitive biases, including the pervasive influence of confirmation bias. Only then can a more informed and nuanced understanding of this enduring mystery emerge. The ultimate answer may remain elusive, but by acknowledging and addressing these psychological factors, we can approach the question of Bigfoot's existence with greater intellectual honesty and integrity.

24

THE ROLE OF SOCIAL AND CULTURAL FACTORS IN BELIEF FORMATION

The enduring fascination with Bigfoot, and the deeply held beliefs surrounding its existence, cannot be understood solely through the lens of individual psychology. Social and cultural factors play a crucial, often overlooked, role in shaping individual convictions. These factors act as powerful currents, influencing the interpretation of evidence, the formation of beliefs, and even the very definition of what constitutes "proof." The narratives surrounding Bigfoot are intricately woven into the fabric of specific cultures and communities, reinforcing existing belief systems and shaping how individuals perceive the ambiguous evidence presented.

For example, indigenous cultures throughout North America have long-standing oral traditions that speak of large, hairy creatures inhabiting the wilderness. These stories, passed down through generations, provide a cultural framework for understanding potential Bigfoot sightings. For members of these communities, the possibility of Bigfoot's existence is not a matter of scientific debate but rather a continuation of their ancestral knowledge. The narratives are not merely tales but a vital part of their cultural identity, lending credence to anecdotal accounts and fostering a sense of connection to the land and its mysterious inhabitants. The weight of this inherited knowledge significantly influences how they approach and interpret any potential evidence related to Bigfoot, making skepticism a foreign concept within this context.

In contrast, the dominant Western scientific worldview often frames Bigfoot as a myth or misidentification. This perspective, rooted in empirical evidence and skepticism, often clashes with the narratives of indigenous communities. This clash highlights the fundamental differences in epistemologies—the ways in which knowledge is acquired and validated—that shape beliefs about Bigfoot. What is considered compelling evidence within one cultural context might be dismissed as anecdotal or insufficient within another. The scientific approach demands rigorous, repeatable evidence, while many indigenous traditions place greater emphasis on oral history and experiential knowledge, leading to divergent interpretations of the same evidence.

The Influence of media also significantly contributes to the social construction of belief. The portrayal of Bigfoot in popular culture, from grainy photographs and blurry videos to fictionalized accounts in books and films, has played a crucial role in shaping public perception. The media, both intentionally and unintentionally, can amplify certain narratives while silencing others. Sensationalized accounts of Bigfoot encounters, often presented without rigorous analysis, can generate excitement and solidify pre-existing beliefs within certain segments of the population. Conversely, critical analyses and debunking efforts, while aiming for objectivity, might be dismissed by those already convinced of Bigfoot's reality, further reinforcing the polarization of opinion.

The role of social groups and communities further amplifies the impact of social and cultural factors. Belief in Bigfoot is often a shared belief, strengthened through social interaction and group validation. Joining a Bigfoot research group, participating in expeditions, or engaging in online forums dedicated to the subject creates a sense of community among believers. Within these social networks, skepticism is often met with resistance, and alternative explanations are dismissed. This social reinforcement solidifies individual beliefs, rendering them more resistant to change even in the face of contradictory evidence. This shared experience and collective validation reinforce individual beliefs, creating a self-perpetuating cycle that strengthens conviction.

The geography of belief Is also a significant factor. Areas with a strong history of Bigfoot sightings, often remote and forested regions, tend to have higher levels of belief within their local populations. The geographical proximity to perceived Bigfoot habitat, coupled with the prevalence of local legends and folklore, contributes to a sense of plausibility and increases the likelihood of individuals accepting accounts of encounters. This regional clustering of belief is a powerful social phenomenon that illustrates how geographical context can shape and reinforce beliefs about Bigfoot, irrespective of the evidence available.

The economic and political factors also intersect with the cultural and social landscape surrounding Bigfoot. In some rural communities, tourism related to Bigfoot sightings can become a significant source of income. Local businesses and individuals can profit from the fascination with Bigfoot, creating a financial incentive for maintaining and even promoting the belief. This economic incentive can shape local narratives and attitudes towards Bigfoot, leading to a self-serving perspective that might downplay or ignore counter-evidence. Similarly, political considerations can influence the way scientific studies and investigations into Bigfoot are approached. Funding for research, media coverage, and official responses are not immune to the influence of political agendas and priorities, further complicating the objective analysis of Bigfoot-related evidence.

Moreover, the historical context surrounding Bigfoot beliefs adds another layer of complexity. The very notion of Bigfoot has shifted and evolved over time, reflecting broader

changes in societal values and scientific understanding. Early accounts often incorporated elements of folklore and mythology, blending real or imagined encounters with existing legends. As scientific methods and technologies advanced, the evidence used to support or refute Bigfoot's existence has also changed, leading to ongoing debates that reflect not only the scientific methodology but also the philosophical shifts in approaches to evidence gathering and evaluation.

Furthermore, the way in which evidence is presented and interpreted varies across cultures. While some cultures may prioritize visual evidence, like photographs or videos, others might rely more on auditory evidence, such as recordings of unusual sounds. This cultural difference in the weighting of different types of evidence can lead to varying levels of conviction regarding the existence of Bigfoot. What might be considered conclusive proof in one cultural framework might be discounted as insufficient in another. This underscores the importance of considering cultural context when evaluating evidence related to Bigfoot.

The psychology of belief and skepticism, as examined in the previous chapter, interacts intricately with these social and cultural dynamics. Confirmation bias, for example, is not merely an individual phenomenon but is also reinforced by the social networks and communities in which individuals operate. The shared interpretation of evidence within these groups strengthens confirmation bias, making it more difficult to challenge deeply held beliefs. Similarly, the social pressures to conform to group norms can lead individuals to suppress their skepticism or to reinterpret contradictory evidence in a way that aligns with the group consensus, further reinforcing the cyclical nature of belief formation within social contexts.

In conclusion, unraveling the complexities of belief in Bigfoot necessitates moving beyond the individual mind and considering the broader social and cultural tapestry that shapes perceptions and interpretations. The influence of indigenous traditions, media representations, social groups, geographical contexts, economic incentives, and political considerations all contribute to the deeply ingrained beliefs surrounding this elusive creature. Understanding these multifaceted factors is crucial for a comprehensive understanding of the enduring enigma of Bigfoot and the compelling psychological and sociological forces that underpin the belief in its existence. A truly comprehensive investigation must acknowledge and analyze these social and cultural contexts to move beyond simplistic explanations of belief formation and towards a nuanced understanding of this persistent mystery.

25

THE PSYCHOLOGY OF DECEPTION
AND HOAXES

The enduring allure of Bigfoot extends beyond the realm of genuine belief; it also fuels the creation of elaborate hoaxes. Understanding the psychology behind these deceptions offers a crucial perspective on the broader phenomenon. Motivations for perpetrating Bigfoot hoaxes are multifaceted and often intertwined. Some hoaxers seek notoriety, aiming for the fleeting spotlight of media attention and the resulting fame, however ephemeral. The thrill of the deception itself, the clever manipulation of public perception, can be a powerful motivator, providing a perverse sense of accomplishment and intellectual superiority. Financial gain is another significant driver; the sale of purported Bigfoot evidence, from blurry photographs to purported footprints, can generate a surprisingly lucrative albeit illicit income stream.

The methods employed in Bigfoot hoaxes vary widely, reflecting the ingenuity (or lack thereof) of the perpetrators. Early hoaxes often relied on crude methods: oversized, artificially created footprints in soft ground, strategically placed branches to simulate movement, and cleverly positioned objects to mimic Bigfoot-like forms in dense vegetation. With the advent of readily available technology, however, hoaxers have gained access to sophisticated tools that can produce increasingly convincing, albeit fabricated, evidence. High-quality digital image manipulation allows for the creation of seemingly authentic photographs and videos, blurring the line between reality and artifice. 3D modeling and printing technologies have enabled the creation of remarkably realistic "Bigfoot" artifacts, further complicating the task of discerning genuine evidence from deliberate fabrication. The ease of digital manipulation also enhances the potential for widespread dissemination of false information, as doxed images and videos can be quickly spread across social media platforms, potentially reaching millions of viewers in a matter of hours.

The psychological Impact of these hoaxes is considerable. They not only erode trust in genuine researchers and their findings but also contribute to a climate of skepticism that hinders serious scientific investigation. The persistent circulation of false evidence makes it harder to distinguish credible accounts from deliberate fabrications, thus undermining the credibility of eyewitness testimonies and potentially delaying genuine breakthroughs. The emotional investment of many Bigfoot enthusiasts further complicates the situation; individuals who firmly believe in Bigfoot's existence may be less receptive to evidence that challenges their deeply held beliefs. This psychological resistance to disconfirming evidence can perpetuate the cycle of deception, as false information reinforces pre-existing biases and strengthens the resilience of misinformation.

The psychology of the *believers* , however, is equally important to consider. Cognitive biases, such as confirmation bias (the tendency to favor information that confirms preexisting beliefs), play a crucial role in how individuals interpret evidence. Once a belief is established, it's remarkably resistant to change, even In the face of overwhelming contradictory evidence. The desire for wonder, for the extraordinary, can also drive belief in Bigfoot, even when rational explanations exist. This yearning for the unknown, for a glimpse into a world beyond the ordinary, taps into a fundamental human need for meaning and mystery. Furthermore, the social aspect of belief is substantial; the collective affirmation within a community of Bigfoot enthusiasts strengthens individual beliefs and reinforces resistance to skepticism. Social media echo chambers amplify these effects, surrounding believers with a constant stream of information that confirms their preconceptions, regardless of its veracity.

Examining historical hoaxes reveals recurring patterns in the methods and motivations of those responsible. Consider the infamous Patterson-Gimlin film, a grainy, albeit compelling, piece of footage purportedly depicting Bigfoot. While its authenticity remains fiercely debated, its persistent influence highlights the enduring power of ambiguous evidence in perpetuating belief. The film's inherent ambiguity, its lack of clear detail, allows for multiple interpretations, each shaping the viewer's preconceptions and beliefs. Similarly, many purported Bigfoot footprints have been shown to be cleverly crafted hoaxes, relying on simple techniques to create convincingly large and unusual tracks. The psychology of these actions involves a degree of self-deception combined with a desire to provoke a reaction, a desire for the resulting impact on public discourse.

It's crucial to distinguish between intentional hoaxes and unintentional misinterpretations. Many reported Bigfoot sightings stem from misidentification of known animals, such as bears or other large mammals. The human tendency to impose patterns and meaning onto ambiguous stimuli, combined with the psychological phenomenon of pareidolia (the perception of patterns or images in random stimuli), can easily lead to misidentifications. This process is amplified by the pre-existing expectation or desire to see Bigfoot, confirming a deeply held belief through misinterpretation of sensory data.

The Investigation of Bigfoot hoaxes necessitates a multidisciplinary approach, combining expertise in psychology, forensic science, and digital forensics. Analyzing the methods employed in hoax creation, identifying the motivations behind these acts, and understanding the impact on public perception all contribute to a more comprehensive understanding of the phenomenon. This requires a rigorous and skeptical approach, capable of critically evaluating purported evidence and distinguishing genuine anomalies from deliberate fabrications. Only through such careful analysis can we hope to unravel the tangled web of belief, deception, and genuine investigation that surrounds the mystery of Bigfoot.

Furthermore, the study of hoaxes provides valuable insights into broader societal trends, such as the spread of misinformation and the influence of social media on belief formation. The ease with which false narratives can spread online, amplified by confirmation bias and echo chambers, highlights the importance of media literacy and critical thinking skills in navigating the information landscape. The study of Bigfoot hoaxes serves as a microcosm of a larger societal issue, demonstrating the power of both deliberate deception and unintentional misinterpretations in shaping collective belief.

The future of Bigfoot research necessitates not only the continued search for physical evidence but also a deeper understanding of the psychological and sociological factors that shape our perception of this elusive creature. This requires a collaborative effort between scientists, psychologists, and anthropologists, working together to analyze the available data with a balanced and critical approach. By acknowledging the role of human psychology in both belief and deception, we can move closer to a more nuanced understanding of the enigma of Bigfoot, embracing both the mystery and the science involved. The persistent existence of hoaxes, while frustrating to genuine investigators, provides valuable case studies that enrich our understanding of human behavior, belief formation, and the enduring power of the mysterious. The combination of scientific rigor and psychological insight is crucial for discerning reality from fabrication in the ongoing saga of Bigfoot. Only by understanding the motivations behind both genuine belief and deliberate deception can we navigate the complex landscape surrounding this enduring mystery.

26

A BALANCED PERSPECTIVE

The enduring mystery of Bigfoot, as we've explored, is fueled by a potent cocktail of eyewitness accounts, purported physical evidence, and the inherent human fascination with the unknown. However, navigating this complex landscape requires a delicate balance between fervent belief and healthy skepticism. Dismissing all claims outright as fabrication risks overlooking potentially significant information, while uncritically accepting every alleged sighting as definitive proof leads to a chaotic and ultimately unproductive pursuit. The path forward necessitates a nuanced approach, one that embraces both the possibility of Bigfoot's existence and the critical evaluation of the evidence supporting that possibility.

Skepticism, in its purest form, is a valuable tool in any scientific inquiry. It demands rigorous testing of evidence, a thorough examination of methodologies, and a healthy dose of doubt before accepting any claim as definitive truth. In the context of Bigfoot research, skepticism acts as a crucial filter, separating genuine leads from fabricated evidence, credible eyewitness accounts from misinterpretations or outright hoaxes. It challenges researchers to refine their methods, to seek more robust data, and to consider alternative explanations before jumping to conclusions. Without this critical lens, the field risks becoming overrun with unsubstantiated claims, hindering the pursuit of verifiable knowledge.

However, unwavering skepticism can also be a significant obstacle. An overly critical approach, devoid of openmindedness, can lead to the dismissal of valuable information or the premature abandonment of promising leads. The very nature of cryptozoology, dealing with elusive and often cryptic subjects, necessitates a certain degree of flexibility and willingness to entertain possibilities that might initially seem improbable. To simply dismiss all anecdotal evidence as unreliable, for example, ignores the potential for valuable insights hidden within seemingly unreliable accounts. Many eyewitness accounts, while lacking in scientific rigor, might still contain crucial details about behavior, habitat, or physical characteristics that can inform future investigations. Discarding these accounts entirely might inadvertently lead to overlooking crucial clues.

The reconciliation of belief and skepticism lies not in choosing one over the other, but in finding a synthesis between the two. This means embracing a cautious optimism, a willingness to explore possibilities while maintaining a rigorous standard of evidence evaluation. It requires a constant reevaluation of existing evidence, a willingness to update beliefs in the face of new information, and a recognition that the pursuit of knowledge is an iterative process. This process is not about definitively proving or disproving Bigfoot's existence, but rather about continually refining our understanding of the phenomenon, based on the most rigorous data analysis available.

This balanced approach requires a multidisciplinary perspective. Zoologists, biologists, anthropologists, psychologists, and even computer scientists can all contribute valuable insights. Zoologists can assess the plausibility of Bigfoot's purported physical characteristics and its ecological niche. Biologists can analyze purported genetic evidence, if any, and assess its validity. Anthropologists can explore the cultural significance of Bigfoot in various indigenous communities, gleaning information about its historical presence in certain regions.

Psychologists can provide valuable insights into the cognitive biases that influence eyewitness accounts and the motivations behind both genuine belief and deliberate deception. Computer scientists can analyze data obtained from various sources, improving the detection of patterns and anomalies in visual or audio recordings. This collaborative approach, merging diverse expertise, is crucial to avoiding the pitfalls of overly simplistic interpretations and to creating a richer, more robust understanding of the phenomenon.

Moreover, technological advancements are playing an increasingly crucial role in addressing the challenges inherent in Bigfoot research. High-resolution cameras, sophisticated audio recording equipment, and DNA analysis techniques are steadily improving the quality and reliability of data collection. The use of drones and remote sensing technology allows for large-scale surveys of remote and previously inaccessible areas, expanding the scope of investigation. Advancements in image and sound processing software can enhance the analysis of existing evidence, potentially revealing details previously overlooked. The use of artificial intelligence and machine learning algorithms can streamline the analysis of vast datasets, identifying patterns and anomalies that might evade human observation. The development and deployment of such technology represents a major step towards a more evidence-based and less speculation-driven investigation.

The historical context of Bigfoot research Is also crucial In understanding the current state of the debate. Early accounts, often rooted in folklore and indigenous traditions, need to be viewed alongside more recent, technologically-informed investigations. While early accounts may lack the scientific rigor of modern research, they can provide valuable contextual information, shedding light on the long-standing human interaction with this elusive creature. Tracing the evolution of Bigfoot investigations, from anecdotal reports to more sophisticated scientific inquiries, provides a valuable perspective on the shifting methods and evolving understanding of this phenomenon.

Further complicating the picture is the influence of media representation on public perception. The portrayal of Bigfoot in popular culture, from documentaries to fictional films, can significantly shape public belief and understanding. While some portrayals might encourage critical thinking and scientific rigor, others can perpetuate stereotypes and misinformation. A critical analysis of media representation, therefore, is essential to separating genuine information from sensationalized narratives. The power of media narratives cannot be underestimated, influencing the way people interpret evidence and shape their attitudes toward the subject.

Finally, the question of Bigfoot's existence remains open. The absence of definitive proof does not automatically equate to disproof. The elusive nature of the creature, combined with the vast and often inaccessible terrain it allegedly inhabits, makes definitive verification a monumental task. However, this lack of conclusive evidence does not invalidate the ongoing pursuit. The continued investigation of Bigfoot represents not just a search for a specific creature, but also a broader inquiry into the limits of our knowledge, the power of human perception, and the enduring allure of the unknown. The ongoing research, with its blend of rigorous scientific methodology and openminded exploration, continues to challenge our assumptions and deepen our understanding of the natural world, even in the face of persistent uncertainty. The pursuit is a testament to the human spirit's unending curiosity and the persistent search for knowledge, regardless of the challenges and uncertainties involved.

The ongoing saga of Bigfoot demonstrates the Importance of fostering a balanced perspective, one that welcomes both skepticism and a willingness to explore the extraordinary. It reminds us that the pursuit of truth is a complex and iterative process, requiring a constant reassessment of evidence and a collaborative effort across multiple disciplines. Ultimately, the question of Bigfoot's existence is not simply a matter of proving or disproving a hypothesis; it is a powerful metaphor for the ongoing human endeavor to understand the world around us, acknowledging both the limitations of our knowledge and the enduring power of the unknown. The journey of investigation itself, with its challenges and uncertainties, is just as significant as any potential discovery. The ultimate conclusion may remain elusive, but the process enriches our understanding of human psychology, scientific inquiry, and the enduring appeal of mystery. This balanced approach, integrating scientific rigor with an open mind, is the only path towards a truly nuanced and informed understanding of the Bigfoot enigma.

27

FROM FICTION TO DOCUMENTARY

Bigfoot's transition from shadowy folklore to a staple of popular culture is a fascinating journey reflecting societal anxieties, technological advancements, and our enduring fascination with the unknown. Its depiction in literature and film has evolved significantly, moving from early, often simplistic representations in pulp fiction and B-movies to more nuanced portrayals in modern documentaries and independent films. Early fictional accounts frequently presented Bigfoot as a monstrous, often violent creature, embodying primal fears of the wilderness and the unknown. These narratives often capitalized on the inherent mystery surrounding the creature, utilizing exaggerated features and dramatic confrontations to heighten the sense of danger and suspense. Think of the countless low-budget horror films of the 1950s and 60s, where Bigfoot was often a shambling, hairy beast lurking in the woods, a creature easily dispatched with gunfire or a well-placed axe. These depictions served to solidify a particular image of Bigfoot in the collective consciousness – a frightening, albeit somewhat clumsy, antagonist.

The emergence of more sophisticated filmmaking techniques and the rise of the documentary genre brought about a gradual shift in Bigfoot's cinematic portrayal. While the creature still held a position of mystery and elusiveness, the focus shifted towards investigative approaches. Documentaries often presented "evidence" of Bigfoot's existence, such as grainy footage, blurry photographs, and eyewitness testimonies. This approach, while intended to lend an air of legitimacy to the Bigfoot mythos, often fell prey to the limitations of the technology and inherent challenges of verifying eyewitness accounts. The inherent ambiguity surrounding the evidence allowed for both believers and skeptics to interpret the presented material through their own lenses, highlighting the enduring controversy surrounding the creature's existence.

The Patterson-Gimlin film, arguably the most famous piece of alleged Bigfoot footage, significantly impacted Bigfoot's portrayal in both fiction and non-fiction media. Its release in 1967 ignited a renewed wave of interest in Bigfoot, influencing countless books, films, and television programs. The film's ambiguous nature – a creature partially visible, moving with an unsettling gait – fostered endless debate regarding its authenticity, becoming a pivotal point of contention within the Bigfoot community. While its veracity continues to be debated by experts, the film's impact on Bigfoot's cultural narrative is undeniable. Its influence is evident in the way the creature is depicted in numerous films and television shows following its release, establishing a visual benchmark for Bigfoot representations that persists to this day.

In the realm of literature, Bigfoot's literary evolution mirrors its cinematic journey. Early novels and short stories presented Bigfoot as a frightening antagonist, utilizing its size and strength to generate suspense and terror. However, as our understanding of the creature (or the lack thereof) evolved, so too did its literary representation. More recent works often portray Bigfoot with a greater degree of complexity, delving into its potential social behavior, its relationship with the natural world, and the ethical dilemmas surrounding its existence. Some authors have presented Bigfoot as an intelligent, misunderstood creature, challenging the traditional view of it as a mindless monster. Others have incorporated Bigfoot into broader narratives examining themes of environmental conservation, the relationship between humans and nature, and the consequences of encroaching upon unknown territories.

The shift towards more nuanced portrayals is also evident in the growing number of Bigfoot-themed documentaries which strive for a more balanced approach, incorporating both compelling evidence and counterarguments. These productions frequently feature interviews with researchers, scientists, and eyewitnesses, presenting a range of perspectives to engage viewers in the ongoing debate. The increased accessibility of filmmaking technologies has allowed for a more immersive experience, incorporating high-definition footage, advanced sound design, and expert analysis to create a more compelling narrative.

However, the commercialization of Bigfoot has also led to a proliferation of low-quality productions, often capitalizing on the sensational aspects of the legend without contributing meaningfully to the ongoing discussion. These productions sometimes sensationalize encounters and often fall short on credible evidence, relying instead on conjecture and speculation to generate interest. The resulting blurring of lines between fact and fiction highlights the critical importance of approaching Bigfoot-themed media with a discerning eye, evaluating the credibility of sources and assessing the quality of evidence presented.

Bigfoot's cultural significance extends beyond its mere presence in books and films. It has become an iconic figure representing the unknown, the mysteries that still linger in our world, and the allure of the unexplored wilderness. Bigfoot serves as a blank canvas onto which we project our hopes, fears, and societal anxieties. Its continued presence in popular culture, from children's books to high-budget Hollywood films, signifies a deeper engagement with questions of nature, mystery, and the boundaries of our understanding of the world around us. The creature's symbolic resonance extends to themes of environmental conservation, challenging us to reconsider our relationship with nature and to recognize the potential for undiscovered wonders to still exist in the world.

The enduring appeal of bigfoot, however, lies in its elusiveness.

The fact that it remains unconfirmed, existing primarily in anecdotal evidence and tantalizing glimpses, fuels speculation and allows for a wide range of interpretations. This ambiguity fosters continued interest and allows the Bigfoot mythos to adapt and evolve alongside societal changes and technological advancements. The creature's enduring presence in popular culture serves not only as entertainment but also a mirror reflecting our own fascination with the unknown, our persistent desire to explore the uncharted territories of our world, and our ongoing search for answers to the lingering mysteries that remain unsolved. As long as Bigfoot remains elusive, its place in popular culture is guaranteed, continuing to spark debate, inspire creativity, and remind us of the vast unknown that still surrounds us. The evolution of Bigfoot's portrayal in media, from simple horror villain to complex symbol, represents a fascinating reflection of our changing perspectives on the natural world, the power of storytelling, and the persistent allure of the mysterious. Further research into the evolving depiction of Bigfoot in popular culture could explore the intersection of environmentalism and Bigfoot narratives, examining how changing environmental attitudes might influence future representations. This analysis could potentially reveal shifts in our collective understanding of conservation, wilderness preservation, and our responsibility towards unexplored ecosystems.

The impact of social media on Bigfoot's representation also warrants further consideration. The rapid dissemination of information, including eyewitness accounts and alleged photographic evidence, through platforms like YouTube, Twitter, and Facebook, has both expanded and complicated the Bigfoot narrative. While social media enables broader participation in the discussion, it also presents challenges in terms of verifying information and separating credible sources from misinformation. A detailed examination of this interplay between social media, public perception, and the perpetuation of the Bigfoot mythos is critical to understanding the creature's evolving presence in contemporary culture.

Finally, the economic implications of Bigfoot's cultural significance deserve further investigation. The tourism industry, fueled by the legend of Bigfoot, generates revenue for communities located in purported Bigfoot hotspots. The sale of Bigfoot-themed merchandise, from books and films to clothing and souvenirs, also represents a substantial economic activity. A comprehensive analysis of the financial and economic implications of the Bigfoot phenomenon would offer a more complete understanding of its multifaceted impact on society. In conclusion, Bigfoot's journey through literature and film reflects not only the evolution of storytelling techniques and technological advancements but also our enduring fascination with the unknown and our evolving relationship with the natural world. Its continued presence in popular culture serves as a testament to its enduring power as a symbol of mystery, wonder, and the persistent questions that remain unanswered.

28

THE IMPACT OF MEDIA REPRESENTATION ON PUBLIC PERCEPTION

The pervasive influence of media on public perception of Bigfoot cannot be overstated. From early pulp fiction to modern documentaries, the portrayal of this enigmatic creature has dramatically shaped how the general public understands—or misunderstands—its potential existence. The initial depictions often leaned heavily into sensationalism, portraying Bigfoot as a monstrous, aggressive threat, lurking in the shadows of the wilderness. This portrayal, cemented in the public consciousness through low-budget horror films and sensationalized news reports, established a framework of fear and skepticism that persists even today. These early representations often lacked scientific rigor, prioritizing entertainment value over accuracy, thereby fueling misconceptions and reinforcing pre-existing biases.

The transition from these early, simplistic portrayals to more nuanced representations in recent years marks a significant shift in how Bigfoot is presented in the media.

Documentaries, for instance, often attempt to present a more balanced view, incorporating eyewitness accounts alongside scientific analysis of purported evidence. However, even in these more sophisticated presentations, the inherent difficulties of proving or disproving Bigfoot's existence often leads to ambiguity. This ambiguity, while potentially frustrating for those seeking definitive answers, is arguably a reflection of the creature's elusive nature and the challenges inherent in researching such a phenomenon.

The Impact of television, particularly reality shows focusing on Bigfoot investigations, deserves specific attention.

Programs that blend amateur investigations with expert opinions often present a compelling narrative, albeit one that can be susceptible to bias and confirmation bias. The inherent drama and suspense involved in these shows often overshadow the complexities of scientific investigation, potentially leading viewers to prioritize entertainment over critical evaluation of the presented evidence. Furthermore, the editing and presentation styles used in these productions can significantly influence the audience's perception of the credibility of both the evidence and the investigators. A carefully edited sequence emphasizing suggestive sounds or blurry images can create a stronger impression of Bigfoot's presence than a more measured presentation of the available data.

The Internet and social media have further complicated the narrative surrounding Bigfoot. The ease of sharing information, both credible and dubious, has resulted in a proliferation of eyewitness accounts, purported evidence, and speculative theories. While the internet provides a valuable platform for disseminating information and facilitating discussions amongst researchers and enthusiasts, it also serves as a breeding ground for misinformation and the amplification of unsubstantiated claims. The viral nature of compelling (though often inaccurate) footage or images can significantly impact public opinion, creating a self-perpetuating cycle of speculation and misinterpretation. Discerning credible information from fabricated accounts requires a high degree of critical thinking and media literacy, a skill not always readily available to the average viewer.

The role of documentaries in shaping public perception is complex. While some documentaries strive for objectivity, presenting a balanced view of the evidence and the arguments surrounding Bigfoot's existence, others prioritize narrative storytelling over scientific rigor. The emotional impact of witnessing purported eyewitness accounts, coupled with dramatic reenactments, can powerfully influence viewers' opinions, even if the scientific validity of the presented evidence is questionable. The choice of experts interviewed, the focus of the narrative, and the overall tone of the documentary significantly influence the message conveyed to the audience. A documentary highlighting the skepticism of scientists, for example, can have a dramatically different effect on the viewer than a documentary that primarily features the testimonies of believers.

Furthermore, the enduring popularity of Bigfoot in popular culture extends beyond television and documentaries. Bigfoot's image is pervasive in various forms of merchandise, from T-shirts and mugs to action figures and video games. This widespread commercialization further solidifies the creature's cultural significance and helps to maintain its presence in the public consciousness. However, this commercialization also raises questions about the potential for exploitation of the legend for purely economic gain, potentially blurring the lines between legitimate investigation and the creation of a marketable commodity.

The media's depiction of Bigfoot often reflects and reinforces pre-existing societal anxieties and beliefs. The creature serves as a powerful symbol, representing both the unknown and our relationship with the natural world. In times of environmental concern and ecological uncertainty, the mystery of Bigfoot can resonate deeply with individuals who yearn for a connection to something beyond the confines of human civilization. This emotional connection, fueled by media portrayals, can significantly influence perceptions and beliefs, even in the absence of conclusive evidence.

The economic impact of Bigfoot's media presence is significant. Towns and communities in areas where purported Bigfoot sightings are frequent often leverage the legend to attract tourists, boosting local economies through tourism-related businesses. The creation and sale of Bigfoot themed merchandise also contribute to a substantial economic activity. This economic dimension reinforces the creature's cultural significance, creating a feedback loop where the media's representation of Bigfoot not only influences public perception but also generates economic benefits that, in turn, perpetuate the legend's continued presence in popular culture.

In conclusion, the relationship between media representation and public perception of Bigfoot is multifaceted and complex. The media, through its various forms, has shaped how generations understand and perceive this enigmatic creature, often prioritizing entertainment value over scientific rigor. While some media outlets strive for a balanced approach, others perpetuate misinformation and sensationalized narratives. Understanding the media's impact is crucial for critically evaluating the information available and forming well-informed opinions about this enduring mystery. The challenge lies in navigating the often blurred lines between credible investigation, sensationalized storytelling, and the commercial exploitation of a cultural icon. The future of understanding Bigfoot, therefore, necessitates not only continued scientific investigation but also a critical engagement with the ways in which media representations shape our collective understanding of this fascinating enigma.

29

ANALYZING THE PORTRAYAL OF BIGFOOT IN DIFFERENT GENRES

The evolution of Bigfoot's image across various media genres reveals a fascinating case study in cultural appropriation and the power of narrative. Early portrayals, largely confined to pulp fiction and newspaper accounts of the 1950s and 60s, frequently depicted Bigfoot as a terrifying, almost monstrous figure. These narratives, often rooted in sensationalism, served to heighten the mystery and fuel public fascination, but rarely aimed for nuanced or realistic depictions. Bigfoot was the ultimate "other," a lurking threat in the untamed wilderness, a symbol of primal fear and the unknown. This early depiction, cemented in the public imagination through grainy photographs and exaggerated eyewitness accounts, profoundly shaped subsequent interpretations.

The low-budget horror films of this era, often capitalizing on the burgeoning interest in cryptids, solidified this image. Bigfoot was invariably portrayed as a hairy, hulking brute, capable of immense strength and violence. These films, while rarely sophisticated in their storytelling or visual effects, proved incredibly effective in embedding a specific image of Bigfoot within popular culture. Think of the countless B-movies where the creature was little more than a furry monster, a plot device designed to create scares and generate box office revenue. The emphasis on fear and violence largely eclipsed any attempt at scientific plausibility, reinforcing the notion of Bigfoot as a creature of myth and legend, rather than a potential subject of scientific investigation.

The transition into the 70s and 80s saw a subtle shift, although the monstrous image largely persisted. Television shows and documentaries, while still often engaging in sensationalism, began to incorporate elements of investigative journalism. These programs frequently featured interviews with alleged eyewitnesses, presenting purported evidence and attempting to build a case for Bigfoot's existence. However, the line between genuine investigation and entertainment often remained blurred. The focus remained on the mystery and thrill of the chase, rather than a rigorous, scientific approach. This period marked the beginning of a more complex portrayal of Bigfoot, moving beyond simplistic horror to encompass a broader range of narrative possibilities. The creature became less a mindless monster and more of an elusive enigma, a symbol of the unexplored depths of the wilderness.

The rise of more sophisticated filmmaking techniques In later decades allowed for a further evolution of Bigfoot's onscreen persona. While the monstrous depiction persisted in low-budget horror films, other genres began to experiment with alternative representations. Some documentaries adopted a more skeptical approach, questioning the validity of existing evidence and highlighting the possibility of misidentification or hoaxing. Others strived for a more balanced presentation, exploring the arguments for and against Bigfoot's existence without overtly favoring one side.

The advent of CGI also transformed the usual depiction of Bigfoot. No longer constrained by the limitations of practical effects, filmmakers could now create more realistic and nuanced portrayals. This led to a greater range of interpretations, some still terrifying, but others depicting Bigfoot as a more majestic, almost noble creature. The creature became less of a simple "monster" and more of a complex symbol, capable of representing different aspects of nature, mystery, and the unexplored potential of the natural world.

Literary representations of Bigfoot have mirrored this evolution. Early fictional accounts frequently emphasized the fearsome aspects of the creature, employing Bigfoot as a plot device to create suspense and horror. More recent novels and short stories, however, have adopted a more complex approach, exploring the creature's potential place within the ecological landscape and examining the philosophical implications of its existence. These works often delved into the ethical implications of human interaction with cryptids, highlighting the potential consequences of encroachment on the creature's habitat and the importance of respecting the mysteries of the natural world.

The role of Bigfoot in children's literature provides a further illustration of this nuanced shift in portrayal. Early portrayals often leaned towards the fearsome and monstrous, but contemporary works often present Bigfoot as a more benevolent figure, a gentle giant inhabiting the wilderness. This change reflects a broader trend in children's literature towards presenting fantastical creatures in a more positive and approachable light, fostering a sense of wonder and curiosity rather than fear. This shift aligns with a broader cultural movement towards greater environmental awareness and respect for the natural world. Bigfoot, once a symbol of fear, is now, in some contexts, a symbol of environmental conservation and the untouched wilderness.

The Internet and social media have further complicated the portrayal of Bigfoot, creating a vast and often chaotic landscape of information, misinformation, and speculation. Websites, blogs, and online forums dedicated to Bigfoot provide a platform for enthusiasts to share their experiences, evidence, and theories. However, this accessibility also means that unsubstantiated claims and outright hoaxes can easily spread, making it challenging to discern credible information from unreliable sources. The online environment has democratized the narrative around Bigfoot, allowing for a multiplicity of voices and perspectives, but also fostering a climate of confusion and polarization. The challenge lies in navigating this vast digital landscape, critically evaluating the information available, and seeking out reliable sources of evidence.

This digital age has also given rise to a new form of Bigfoot narrative: the meme. Bigfoot's image is frequently appropriated and repurposed in internet humor, often stripped of its original context and transformed into a symbol of absurdity, awkwardness, or unexpected encounters. This underscores the multifaceted nature of Bigfoot's cultural significance, moving beyond the realms of fear and scientific investigation to occupy a space in popular culture as a symbol of the unexpected and the strangely humorous. The casual appropriation of Bigfoot's image in memes shows the creature's enduring presence in the collective consciousness, even as its depiction is constantly being reinterpreted and redefined.

Analyzing the diverse portrayals of Bigfoot across different media genres reveals a complex and evolving relationship between cultural representation and public perception. The creature, once primarily a symbol of fear and the unknown, has become a multifaceted icon, representing various aspects of nature, mystery, and the human fascination with the unexplained. The continued evolution of Bigfoot's image across different media underscores its enduring cultural significance and capacity to adapt and change along with the evolving media landscape itself. Understanding the shifts in these portrayals offers crucial insight into how we, as a society, grapple with the unknown, and how our perceptions are shaped not only by evidence, but also by the narratives we choose to tell and believe. The future of Bigfoot in popular culture, therefore, remains as enigmatic as the creature itself. The diverse and often conflicting portrayals continue to shape public perception, forcing us to critically examine the lines between credible investigation, sensationalized storytelling, and the enduring power of myth and legend. The ultimate truth about Bigfoot, if such a truth exists, may remain elusive, but the exploration of its image across various media provides a rich and fascinating lens through which to understand the nature of mystery, belief, and the cultural significance of the unexplained.

30

TOURISM AND MERCHANDISE

The cultural impact of Bigfoot extends far beyond the realm of film and literature; it has become a significant player in the tourism and merchandise industries. The very existence of Bigfoot, whether confirmed or not, fuels a substantial economic engine, particularly in regions where alleged sightings are most frequent. Towns and communities in the Pacific Northwest, for example, have capitalized on the legend, creating Bigfoot-themed attractions, festivals, and events that draw in tourists from across the globe. These attractions range from small, locally-owned roadside stands selling Bigfoot-themed trinkets to larger, organized events featuring guest speakers, researchers, and even purported Bigfoot experts.

The economic impact Is undeniable. Hotels, restaurants, and other local businesses experience a surge in revenue during these events, contributing significantly to the local economies. The creation of dedicated Bigfoot museums and visitor centers further solidifies the commercialization of the legend, providing a focal point for enthusiasts and generating consistent revenue streams. These ventures often combine elements of genuine investigation and local folklore with commercial appeal, often blurring the lines between serious research and entertainment. While some might criticize this commercialization as trivializing the pursuit of evidence, proponents argue it highlights the enduring cultural fascination with Bigfoot and provides a financial incentive for maintaining the legend, supporting ongoing research, and preserving local traditions tied to the creature.

The merchandise associated with Bigfoot is equally diverse and lucrative. From t-shirts and mugs to books and action figures, the range of Bigfoot-themed products is vast. Online marketplaces and dedicated Bigfoot shops are overflowing with items catering to every level of enthusiast, from casual observers to serious collectors. The visual representation of Bigfoot varies greatly, ranging from the terrifying, monstrous depiction of early pulp fiction to more cartoonish, playful versions designed for children's merchandise. This adaptation reflects the complex and often contradictory images of Bigfoot that exist in popular culture, highlighting the ongoing negotiation between the mystery and the commercial. The availability and popularity of this merchandise indicate a broad public engagement with the legend, far beyond the dedicated researchers and cryptozoologists. This commercial success, in a sense, reflects the enduring power of the Bigfoot narrative itself.

The creation of specific "Bigfoot hotspots" is a crucial aspect of this commercialization. Areas where alleged sightings have occurred, or where purported evidence has been found, are often transformed into tourist destinations. This frequently involves the development of hiking trails, viewing platforms, and interpretative centers designed to enhance the visitor experience. While some might view these efforts as merely capitalizing on a myth, it's worth noting that this process can indirectly contribute to the preservation of natural landscapes and the promotion of eco-tourism. The economic incentives created by Bigfoot-related tourism might, in some cases, encourage environmental protection and sustainable practices in areas otherwise at risk of exploitation. However, this benefit is not universally guaranteed and requires careful management to prevent environmental damage from unchecked tourism.

The line between legitimate research and commercial exploitation often blurs within the context of Bigfoot tourism. Some enterprises successfully combine serious investigation with entertaining displays. They may present documented accounts alongside speculative interpretations, giving visitors a nuanced perspective on the evidence while still maintaining a sense of wonder and mystery. This balanced approach can be highly effective in engaging a broad audience and generating financial support for ongoing research. However, a critical approach is still necessary to identify instances where commercial interests overshadow scientific rigor, presenting conjecture as fact or exploiting public fascination for profit without contributing meaningful information.

It's also Important to consider the ethical Implications of commercializing Bigfoot. The very act of marketing the legend can inadvertently promote misleading information or fuel misconceptions about the creature. The desire to profit from the legend could lead to fabricated encounters or exaggerated claims, ultimately hindering genuine investigation. Furthermore, the commodification of Bigfoot risks reducing a complex and fascinating mystery to a simplistic and easily marketable product, potentially diminishing its cultural significance and undermining serious efforts to unravel the truth behind the legend.

Beyond the immediate economic impact, the commercialization of Bigfoot has had a significant cultural effect. The widespread availability of Bigfoot-related products permeates popular culture, subtly embedding the legend into the fabric of daily life. For example, the casual inclusion of Bigfoot imagery in everyday items such as coffee mugs or t-shirts normalizes the idea of the creature, making it a more readily accepted element of societal discourse. This normalization, while seemingly trivial, can have a significant impact on how people approach the subject of Bigfoot. It softens the stigma associated with believing in the creature, leading to more open and less judgmental conversations about the possibility of its existence.

Furthermore, the cultural impact extends beyond the simple

presence of merchandise. The creation of Bigfoot-themed events and festivals actively constructs a community around the legend. These gatherings bring together individuals with a shared interest, providing a space for discussion, storytelling, and the exchange of information. This sense of community, built around the mystery of Bigfoot, creates a network of support and validation for those who believe in the creature's existence, strengthening their conviction and furthering the legend's endurance. This shared sense of belief and curiosity is a powerful force, sustaining the legend and contributing to its continued presence in popular culture.

The commercialization of Bigfoot, however complex and ethically nuanced, is an undeniable facet of its cultural impact. It reveals the enduring fascination with the legend, demonstrating its power to drive tourism, generate merchandise sales, and foster a sense of community among believers. The economic success of Bigfoot-themed businesses showcases the potent narrative power of the mystery itself. This economic impact is not solely a negative phenomenon. While it's crucial to maintain a critical perspective on the potential for exploitation and misinformation, the positive economic effects of Bigfoot-related tourism and merchandise in certain regions are undeniable, often stimulating local economies and preserving natural areas.

However, careful consideration must be given to the balance between commercial gain and responsible stewardship of the legend. The ethical considerations surrounding the potential for misinformation and the commodification of a potentially genuine scientific mystery cannot be ignored. Striking a balance between capitalizing on the enduring appeal of Bigfoot and maintaining scientific integrity remains a significant challenge for all stakeholders involved, from researchers and local businesses to the consumers themselves. Ultimately, the future of Bigfoot in popular culture, and its continued commercial success, hinges on responsible management and a critical awareness of the complex interplay between myth, reality, and profit. The story of Bigfoot's commercialization is, therefore, far more intricate than simply a tale of merchandising; it's a reflection of our enduring fascination with the unknown and the complex ways in which we engage with legend and lore in our modern world. The careful consideration of these ethical and economic implications will shape the future of Bigfoot's role in popular culture and the manner in which we approach the search for answers regarding its existence.

31

SYMBOLISM AND ICONOGRAPHY

B eyond the economic impact, Bigfoot's cultural significance lies
in its potent symbolism and enduring presence in modern folklore. The creature transcends mere myth; it represents a powerful
archetype tapping into deep-seated human anxieties and desires. Its
elusive nature fuels our fascination with the unknown, a primal
curiosity that has driven exploration and discovery throughout
history. The very notion of a large, unclassified primate roaming the
wilderness challenges our understanding of the natural world and
our place within it. This challenges the established scientific para-
digms and our anthropocentric worldview, suggesting the possibility
of undiscovered species and unexplored ecological niches.

Bigfoot's symbolism often reflects a connection to nature and the
untamed wilderness. In many Native American traditions, similar
creatures hold significant spiritual meaning, often representing
powerful forces of nature or guardians of the forest. These interpretations vary widely across different tribes and nations, demonstrating
the complex and multifaceted nature of Bigfoot's symbolic representation within indigenous cultures. The creature's large size and
strength can be interpreted as a symbol of raw power and untamed
energy, while its elusiveness hints at the mysteries and secrets that

remain hidden within the natural world. These interpretations are not static; they evolve and adapt as societal perceptions of nature and wilderness shift.

The enduring presence of Bigfoot in popular culture also reflects our fascination with the uncanny and the mysterious. The creature embodies the "liminal" space between the known and the unknown, the familiar and the extraordinary.

This liminal quality makes Bigfoot particularly appealing to those who seek to challenge established norms and question accepted realities. Bigfoot's existence, or the lack thereof, serves as a blank canvas onto which we project our own anxieties, hopes, and desires. Is it a reflection of our fear of the unknown, or a symbol of hope for the preservation of untamed wilderness? This ambiguity contributes to its continued relevance in discussions about environmentalism, scientific inquiry, and the boundaries of human knowledge.

The Iconography of Bigfoot Is equally intriguing. From grainy photographs and blurry video footage to detailed artistic renderings, the visual representation of the creature

has evolved alongside our understanding (or misunderstanding) of it. Early depictions often relied on eyewitness accounts, frequently resulting in inconsistent representations of the creature's physical attributes. This inconsistency itself highlights the challenges of interpreting anecdotal evidence, and the difficulties involved in capturing a fleeting glimpse of a potentially elusive creature. The variations in physical descriptions – from hairy bipeds to more ape-like forms – further reflect the subjective nature of eyewitness testimony and the limitations of observational data in cryptozoological investigations.

The evolution of Bigfoot's visual representation is also influenced by artistic interpretations and popular media portrayals. In film and literature, Bigfoot's appearance is often adjusted to fit the narrative needs and audience expectations of the particular medium. While some portrayals attempt to maintain a degree of realism, based on available (albeit limited) evidence, others embrace a more fantastical or monstrous representation. These creative interpretations highlight the interplay between fact and fiction, science and imagination, within the context of the Bigfoot phenomenon. The resulting imagery – a large, hairy humanoid lurking in the shadows – has become a powerful and instantly recognizable symbol in popular culture, transcending its association with any specific scientific inquiry.

The recurring motif of Bigfoot's footprints adds another layer to the creature's iconography. While often presented as undeniable proof of its existence, the footprints themselves have been subject to scrutiny and debate, with some dismissed as hoaxes or misidentifications. Nevertheless, the image of giant footprints in the mud or snow has become synonymous with Bigfoot, perpetuating the legend and fostering further speculation about the creature's size, weight, and gait. The varying sizes and shapes of purported Bigfoot tracks add to the enigmatic nature of the creature, making it difficult to establish a definitive physical profile based on footprint evidence alone. Despite this ambiguity, the footprint remains a powerful visual symbol that continues to capture the imagination of believers and skeptics alike.

Bigfoot's cultural impact extends beyond visual representations; its presence in music, literature, and other forms of media underscores its enduring appeal. Songs, stories, and poems about Bigfoot contribute to the narrative richness surrounding the creature, shaping its character and perpetuating its legendary status across various cultural contexts. The exploration of Bigfoot in literature ranges from realistic depictions of investigations to fictional accounts that weave the creature into fantastical narratives. The diverse approaches to Bigfoot in creative media highlight the creature's adaptability as a cultural symbol, allowing for interpretations that range from scientific mystery to supernatural folklore. This adaptation demonstrates the creature's ability to resonate with diverse audiences and adapt to evolving cultural interests.

The influence of Bigfoot on the broader cultural landscape should not be overlooked. It's interwoven with themes of environmentalism, challenging our anthropocentric views of the natural world and promoting an awareness of the importance of wilderness preservation. The very existence of an unknown, large primate

surviving undetected in relatively close proximity to human populations underscores the vastness and unexplored aspects of the natural
world. This perception fosters a sense of wonder and reinforces the
importance of conservation efforts. Bigfoot serves as a powerful
metaphor for the fragility of ecosystems and the ongoing need to
protect biodiversity. The mystery of Bigfoot inspires debates on scientific methodology, critical thinking, and the limitations of human
knowledge. It showcases the challenges involved in balancing
rational inquiry with the allure of the unknown.

Furthermore, Bigfoot's pervasiveness in popular culture encourages discussions on the nature of evidence, the reliability of eyewitness accounts, and the challenges involved in studying elusive and
infrequent phenomena. The scrutiny given to alleged Bigfoot
evidence, including footprints, hair samples, and video footage, highlights the importance of rigorous scientific methodology and the
need for critical assessment of potentially biased or unreliable data.
Bigfoot's cultural significance extends to its influence on scientific
practices, promoting more rigorous analytical approaches to the
study of rare phenomena and the limitations of relying solely on
anecdotal evidence.

The role of folklore and mythology in shaping Bigfoot's cultural
significance cannot be ignored. Tales of large, hairy humanoids have
existed for centuries in various cultures around the world, suggesting
a deeper, possibly universal, cultural archetype. These stories often
reflect deep-seated beliefs about nature, the supernatural, and the
boundaries between the human and animal worlds. The persistence
of these legends across generations and cultures suggests a powerful
cultural force at play, one that transcends regional and temporal
boundaries. By understanding the historical and cultural contexts of
these stories, we gain a deeper appreciation for the roots of the
Bigfoot legend and its enduring appeal.

In conclusion, Bigfoot's cultural significance is multifaceted and
dynamic. It is not merely a creature of myth, but a potent symbol that
embodies our fascination with the unknown, our relationship with
nature, and the enduring power of folklore. Its presence in popular

culture reflects our collective anxieties and hopes, our yearning for exploration and discovery, and our ongoing quest to understand the world around us. The iconography of Bigfoot – its physical description, its footprints, and its appearance in various media – continues to evolve, reflecting changes in societal attitudes and technological advancements. Its continuing presence in our collective imagination underscores its enduring power as a cultural icon and symbol of enduring mystery. The careful study of Bigfoot's cultural impact provides a unique lens through which to examine our own relationship with the natural world, the limits of human knowledge, and the fascinating interplay between myth, reality, and the human imagination. This continuing exploration offers opportunities for engaging dialogue on scientific methodology, responsible stewardship of our environment, and the enduring appeal of the enigmatic and unexplained.

32

THERMAL INFRARED AND NIGHT VISION

The limitations of traditional observational methods in Bigfoot research are starkly apparent. Eyewitness accounts, while often compelling, are inherently subjective and susceptible to misinterpretation or exaggeration. Photographs and videos, while potentially offering more objective evidence, are frequently blurry, poorly lit, or lack sufficient detail for definitive identification. The nocturnal and elusive nature of the purported creature further compounds these challenges. Fortunately, the rapid advancement of imaging technologies offers a promising new avenue for Bigfoot research, potentially overcoming some of these long-standing hurdles. Thermal, infrared, and night vision technologies, in particular, offer a powerful toolkit for researchers operating in the challenging environments where Bigfoot is most often reported.

Thermal imaging, which detects infrared radiation emitted by objects, provides a unique capability. Unlike visible light cameras, thermal cameras can "see" heat signatures, regardless of ambient light levels. This means researchers can effectively monitor areas at night or in dense forest cover, conditions that previously hampered observation. A warm-blooded creature like Bigfoot would leave a distinct thermal signature against the cooler background of the surrounding environment. By carefully analyzing thermal imagery, researchers can identify potential anomalies—heat signatures that don't correspond to known animals or environmental factors—that warrant further investigation. The high resolution of modern thermal cameras also allows for a more detailed analysis of the size and shape of a heat signature, potentially offering clues about the creature's size and posture. However, it's crucial to note that thermal images are not foolproof. Other sources of heat, such as rocks warmed by the sun or decaying vegetation, can produce false positives. Careful analysis and cross-referencing with other data sources are essential to avoid misinterpretations.

Infrared imaging operates on a similar principle to thermal imaging, detecting infrared radiation. However, infrared cameras often have a broader spectral range and can be sensitive to different wavelengths of infrared light. This wider range can be advantageous in certain circumstances, potentially revealing details not visible in standard thermal imagery. For example, some infrared cameras can penetrate foliage to a greater extent than thermal cameras, allowing researchers to potentially observe a creature obscured by vegetation. Specialized infrared cameras can also be used to analyze the reflective properties of surfaces, a technique that could potentially be used to detect unusual materials or structures associated with Bigfoot. Again, careful calibration and interpretation are crucial, as factors like atmospheric conditions and the reflectivity of different materials can influence the images produced.

Night vision technology, while less directly related to detecting heat signatures, enhances the ability to observe in low-light conditions. Night vision devices amplify available light (including starlight and moonlight) to create visible images, allowing researchers to monitor areas at night without disturbing the environment with artificial illumination. The use of night vision significantly increases the probability of observing nocturnal activity. However, the effectiveness of night vision is dependent on ambient light levels, and heavily forested areas might still present significant challenges. Furthermore, night vision can be susceptible to interference from other light sources, such as vehicle headlights or moonlight reflecting off surfaces.

The effective integration of these technologies requires careful planning and execution. For instance, researchers might deploy a network of strategically placed thermal and infrared cameras to monitor a particular area of interest. The data gathered by these cameras can then be analyzed using specialized software to identify potential Bigfoot sightings. Night vision equipment could supplement this approach, allowing researchers to conduct direct observations in conjunction with the camera systems. Data from these technologies should ideally be integrated with other data sources, such as acoustic recordings and eyewitness accounts, to build a more comprehensive understanding of potential Bigfoot activity.

The successful application of these technologies also depends on careful consideration of environmental factors. Temperature variations, humidity, and atmospheric conditions can all affect the quality of thermal and infrared imagery. Researchers need to understand these factors and compensate for them during data analysis. Similarly, the use of night vision equipment requires careful planning to avoid light pollution and other sources of interference.

Beyond the hardware itself, the analysis of the data presents further challenges. The sheer volume of data generated by these technologies can be overwhelming, requiring sophisticated software and expertise to effectively analyze. Sophisticated image processing techniques and machine learning algorithms might play a crucial role in this process, automatically identifying potential anomalies and prioritizing areas for further investigation. The development of robust algorithms that can distinguish between genuine Bigfoot sightings and false positives remains a significant challenge, requiring further research and development.

Moreover, the ethical considerations surrounding the use of these advanced imaging technologies cannot be ignored. Researchers must ensure their activities do not disturb the natural environment or threaten the privacy of any individuals or animals in the area.

Obtaining the necessary permits and adhering to strict protocols for data collection and analysis are essential.

The application of thermal, infrared, and night vision technologies is not without its limitations. The cost of acquiring and maintaining this sophisticated equipment can be prohibitive for many researchers, limiting access to these valuable tools. Furthermore, the interpretation of data remains a subjective process, requiring expert knowledge and experience. Despite these challenges, the potential benefits are substantial. The use of advanced imaging technologies represents a significant step forward in Bigfoot research, offering a potentially more objective and effective way to investigate this elusive creature. As technology continues to advance, we can expect even more sophisticated tools to emerge, further enhancing the possibilities for future investigation and potentially bringing us closer to understanding the enigma of Bigfoot. The combination of these advanced imaging techniques with other investigative approaches, such as eDNA analysis and AI-powered data analysis, presents an unprecedented opportunity to advance Bigfoot research beyond its current limitations and, perhaps, finally provide definitive answers to some of its most enduring questions. The future of Bigfoot research, therefore, is inextricably linked to technological advancements, promising a more scientific and data-driven approach to this long-standing mystery.

33

A NEW FRONTIER IN DETECTION

The limitations of traditional methods in Bigfoot research—eyewitness accounts, blurry photographs, and anecdotal evidence—have fueled skepticism for decades. However, the advent of environmental DNA (eDNA) analysis offers a revolutionary approach, potentially bypassing the inherent subjectivity and limitations of previous techniques. eDNA, the genetic material shed by organisms into their environment (skin cells, hair, saliva, feces), represents a powerful new tool in the search for definitive proof of Bigfoot's existence. By analyzing soil, water, or even air samples collected from reported Bigfoot habitats, researchers can potentially identify unique genetic signatures that could confirm or refute the presence of an unknown hominin species.

The application of eDNA in wildlife research has already yielded remarkable results. Scientists have successfully used eDNA to detect elusive and endangered species, often in areas where traditional methods have proven ineffective. For example, researchers have successfully identified rare fish species in waterways by extracting DNA from water samples, providing valuable data for conservation efforts. Similar techniques have been utilized to monitor populations of endangered tigers and elephants, effectively assessing population size and distribution without the need for physically observing the animals. These successes demonstrate the sensitivity and potential of eDNA analysis, raising the possibility of similar applications in the search for Bigfoot.

However, applying eDNA analysis to Bigfoot presents unique challenges. The low density of the potential population and the vast, often inaccessible, terrains where Bigfoot is reportedly sighted dramatically increases the difficulty of obtaining viable samples. Furthermore, environmental factors, such as bacterial decomposition and UV radiation, can degrade eDNA, rendering it undetectable after a certain period. The specific environmental conditions within Bigfoot habitats, which are often characterized by dense forest cover, high humidity, and varying soil types, require careful consideration of sample collection and preservation protocols.

The sampling strategy is critical. Researchers would need to develop a rigorous sampling protocol, carefully considering the potential habitats and behavior of Bigfoot. Strategic placement of sampling locations based on reported sightings, known trails, and areas with high potential for habitat use will be crucial for maximizing the likelihood of obtaining relevant samples. The number of samples collected must be sufficient to cover a large geographical area and account for the potential scattering of eDNA over time and environmental conditions. The use of appropriate sampling techniques, including careful handling and preservation of samples to prevent contamination, is equally important.

The laboratory analysis of eDNA presents additional challenges. The process involves extracting and purifying DNA from environmental samples, a complex procedure that requires specialized equipment and expertise. Once extracted, the DNA must be amplified using polymerase chain reaction (PCR) techniques to generate sufficient quantities for sequencing. This step requires careful calibration to avoid contamination and false positives. Following amplification, the DNA is sequenced to determine its genetic code. This data is then compared to existing databases of known species to identify any potential matches or discrepancies. Any unknown sequences, or sequences that don't match known species, require careful analysis and interpretation by experienced geneticists.

The interpretation of the results is potentially the most challenging step. Even if a novel genetic sequence is identified, establishing its connection to Bigfoot requires careful consideration of various factors. It is crucial to rule out potential sources of contamination, such as human DNA or DNA from other known animals. Furthermore, a single positive result doesn't conclusively prove the existence of Bigfoot. Multiple independent samples from different locations and time periods are necessary to build a more robust and convincing case. Statistical analysis of the data is vital to determine the significance of the findings and rule out any possibility of chance occurrence.

The cost of conducting comprehensive eDNA analysis is a significant consideration. The process involves specialized equipment, skilled personnel, and extensive laboratory analysis, making it a relatively expensive undertaking. Securing funding for such a project requires a commitment from research institutions, government agencies, or private investors. The long-term nature of the research also demands a significant investment of time and resources. A single research expedition will likely be insufficient; a sustained, multi-year investigation is needed to fully leverage the potential of eDNA analysis in Bigfoot research.

Despite these challenges, the potential rewards are significant. A successful eDNA analysis could provide definitive scientific proof of Bigfoot's existence, revolutionizing our understanding of hominin evolution and potentially altering our understanding of biodiversity itself. Such a discovery would necessitate a re-evaluation of established scientific knowledge and likely trigger a global surge of interest in cryptozoology. The implications extend beyond the confirmation of Bigfoot's existence; it could lead to the discovery of other unknown species and fundamentally change the way we approach biodiversity research.

Beyond the direct detection of Bigfoot, eDNA analysis can provide valuable insights into the creature's habitat use, population size, and dietary habits. By analyzing the composition of eDNA in different areas, researchers could map potential Bigfoot territories and identify critical habitat zones. This information could inform conservation efforts to protect Bigfoot and its habitat, should the creature be confirmed. Similarly, the analysis of dietary components in fecal eDNA could reveal insights into Bigfoot's food sources and foraging behaviors, providing valuable data to understand its ecological niche.

The ethical considerations surrounding eDNA research are also crucial. If Bigfoot's existence is confirmed, the question of how to protect this elusive species and its habitat from human encroachment and exploitation becomes paramount. Appropriate legislation and international cooperation would be needed to safeguard this new species from potential threats. The development of responsible research protocols that minimize disturbance to Bigfoot and its environment is also critical to ensure the ethical conduct of future investigations.

Collaborative efforts are key to the successful application of eDNA technology in Bigfoot research. The integration of eDNA analysis with other investigative tools, such as advanced imaging technologies and AI-powered data analysis, presents a powerful synergistic approach. Sharing of data and expertise among researchers and institutions is crucial to maximizing the impact of this research and avoiding duplication of efforts. Open access to data and findings will facilitate broader scrutiny and verification of results, bolstering the credibility of the research and fostering public trust in the process.

The future of Bigfoot research is undeniably intertwined with technological advancements. While skepticism remains a significant hurdle, the integration of eDNA analysis into the investigative toolkit offers a promising pathway towards a more scientific and robust approach. This approach, coupled with advancements in other areas of technology, offers the potential to move beyond speculation and into a realm of evidence-based investigation. The journey towards definitively answering the question of Bigfoot's existence remains a long one, but with the deployment of cutting-edge technologies such as eDNA analysis, we stand at the threshold of a new era in the search for this enigmatic creature. The potential impact of a confirmed discovery extends far beyond cryptozoology, touching upon fields of biology, genetics, anthropology, and conservation. The next chapter in Bigfoot research promises to be a compelling one, filled with technological advancements and potential breakthroughs that could reshape our understanding of the natural world.

34

ADVANCED TRACKING AND
MONITORING TECHNOLOGIES

B eyond eDNA, the technological landscape offers a plethora of
tools that could revolutionize Bigfoot research. The limitations
of relying solely on eyewitness accounts and ambiguous photographic evidence are well-documented. These methods are inherently subjective and prone to misinterpretation, leading to persistent
skepticism. However, the integration of advanced tracking and monitoring systems offers a more objective, data-driven approach, minimizing the influence of human error and bias.

One significant advancement lies in the realm of remote sensing
technologies. Motion-activated cameras, already a staple in Bigfoot
research, are constantly evolving. Newer models boast higher resolution, improved low-light performance, and longer battery life.
Furthermore, the integration of thermal imaging capabilities allows
for detection even in complete darkness, a crucial advantage given
the creature's purported nocturnal habits. These cameras can be
strategically deployed in suspected Bigfoot habitats, forming a
network of surveillance that provides continuous monitoring over
vast areas. Data collected from these cameras can be analyzed using
sophisticated software, allowing researchers to identify patterns of

movement, habitat preferences, and even individual characteristics of potential Bigfoot subjects.

The use of drones equipped with high-resolution cameras and thermal sensors offers a significant leap forward in aerial surveillance. Drones allow for a broader perspective of the terrain, covering areas inaccessible by foot or traditional methods. Their maneuverability allows for detailed investigation of remote and rugged landscapes, which often form the core of Bigfoot habitats. The ability to survey large areas efficiently is vital, as Bigfoot sightings are often sporadic and geographically dispersed. Furthermore, drones can be equipped with sensors capable of detecting other environmental data that may correlate with Bigfoot activity, such as variations in soil composition, vegetation density, or even subtle changes in atmospheric pressure. This multisensory approach allows for a comprehensive analysis of the environment, potentially providing clues about Bigfoot's presence and behavior that were previously unavailable.

Acoustic monitoring technologies are another promising avenue for investigation. Bigfoot's alleged vocalizations, often described as loud, low-frequency sounds, present a unique challenge. Traditional audio recording equipment often fails to capture these sounds effectively due to their low frequency and the interference of environmental noise. However, advancements in infrasound detection technology offers a solution. Infrasound sensors can pick up these low frequency sounds over long distances, even through dense vegetation. By deploying a network of strategically placed infrasound sensors across a suspected Bigfoot habitat, researchers can monitor the area for potential vocalizations, potentially identifying communication patterns or even tracking the creature's movements based on the direction of the sound.

Furthermore, the integration of artificial intelligence (AI) and machine learning algorithms is revolutionizing the analysis of data collected from these various sensors. AI can sift through vast amounts of data, identifying subtle patterns or anomalies that might escape human observation. For example, an AI system could be trained to differentiate between the sounds of Bigfoot's alleged vocalizations and other environmental sounds, drastically improving the accuracy of acoustic monitoring. Similarly, AI could be used to analyze images and videos captured by remote cameras, identifying potential Bigfoot sightings or footprints that might be missed by the human eye. The potential for AI to enhance the analysis of data collected from multiple sensors – cameras, drones, acoustic sensors – offers a powerful approach to integrating data from different sources into a coherent picture.

Satellite imagery and Geographic Information Systems (GIS) play a critical role in establishing a baseline understanding of Bigfoot habitat. Satellite images can be used to map vegetation density, elevation changes, and water sources within large geographic areas. This information can be integrated into GIS software to create detailed models of potential Bigfoot habitats, focusing research efforts on areas most likely to support the creature's survival. The integration of historical data on Bigfoot sightings with this detailed habitat modeling can identify areas of high probability for future sightings, directing researchers towards specific locations for intensive field investigation using the aforementioned monitoring technologies.

Beyond the technological advancements in monitoring, developments in genetic analysis techniques continue to refine our ability to detect and identify traces of Bigfoot. While eDNA analysis represents a significant breakthrough, the challenge remains in distinguishing Bigfoot's genetic material from other similar species. Advances in next generation sequencing and bioinformatics offer more sophisticated methods to analyze eDNA samples, increasing the likelihood of detecting even minute amounts of genetic material with higher accuracy. Moreover, improvements in database searching techniques and the development of more sensitive and specific assays allow researchers to compare newly discovered genetic sequences against broader databases, enhancing the likelihood of identifying a novel hominin lineage.

The development of advanced sensor fusion technologies represents a pivotal step forward. Sensor fusion involves the integration of data from multiple sensor systems to create a more complete and accurate understanding of a given situation. By combining data from cameras, acoustic sensors, thermal imaging, and even environmental sensors like soil moisture probes, researchers can generate a more holistic picture of Bigfoot habitat and activity. Sophisticated algorithms are employed to combine data from disparate sources, reducing noise and uncertainty. This approach minimizes the reliance on individual sensor readings, offering a more robust and reliable picture of what's happening in a specific area.

However, technological advancements alone cannot solve the Bigfoot mystery. Ethical considerations are paramount. Respect for wildlife and the environment must be prioritized in all research efforts. The use of drones and other technologies must adhere to strict regulations and guidelines to avoid disturbing animal behavior or causing ecological damage. Collaboration among researchers is essential to share data, resources, and best practices, ensuring that the use of technology is both effective and responsible. Open data sharing amongst researchers is equally critical for progress, fostering a collaborative environment where collective knowledge surpasses individual efforts. The transparent sharing of methods, findings, and data will aid in the validation and verification of research findings, reducing skepticism and enhancing the credibility of the field.

Moreover, the public perception of Bigfoot research is heavily influenced by the responsible dissemination of scientific findings. Clear and concise communication of research methodologies and results, as well as the careful consideration of potential biases, are crucial. The narrative surrounding Bigfoot is often intertwined with folklore, speculation, and media sensationalism. A methodical approach, with a strong emphasis on rigorous scientific methodology, is crucial to establish credibility and guide public perception away from unsubstantiated claims. The ultimate goal is not to prove or disprove the existence of Bigfoot but to explore the question systematically and ethically, using the best available tools and techniques. The future of Bigfoot research hinges not only on technological advancements but also on a renewed commitment to scientific rigor, ethical practice, and clear communication.

35

ARTIFICIAL INTELLIGENCE AND MACHINE LEARNING IN BIGFOOT ANALYSIS

The integration of artificial intelligence (AI) and machine learning (ML) presents a transformative opportunity for Bigfoot research, offering the potential to analyze vast datasets far beyond the capacity of human researchers. Traditional methods, reliant on manual examination of blurry photographs, anecdotal evidence, and fragmented physical samples, are inherently limited by human bias and the subjectivity of interpretation. AI and ML, however, can process and analyze data objectively, identifying patterns and correlations that might escape human notice.

One significant application lies in the analysis of auditory data. The distinctive sounds attributed to Bigfoot, ranging from guttural roars to unexplained vocalizations, are often difficult to discern from natural phenomena or human generated noises. AI algorithms, trained on extensive libraries of various soundscapes, can be employed to filter out background noise and isolate potential Bigfoot vocalizations with far greater accuracy than human ears. Furthermore, sophisticated machine learning models can learn to distinguish between different types of calls, potentially revealing patterns related to communication, territoriality, or even different Bigfoot populations. This analysis could also help to pinpoint locations where these sounds are most frequently detected, directing field researchers to areas of higher probability.

Similarly, AI can play a crucial role in analyzing visual data. The abundance of low-quality images and videos purportedly depicting Bigfoot often suffers from poor resolution, lighting conditions, and ambiguous context. AI image recognition and enhancement algorithms can improve the quality of these images, sharpening details, enhancing contrast, and reducing noise. Furthermore, machine learning models trained on a vast database of various animal species can be used to compare and contrast features in images attributed to Bigfoot with known creatures, helping to eliminate misidentifications. Such analysis can not only help to confirm or refute claims of Bigfoot sightings but also lead to a better understanding of the creature's potential morphology and behavior based on consistent visual features extracted from a multitude of blurry or obscured images and videos. The development of AI-powered systems that can identify subtle movement patterns in video footage could also significantly enhance research efforts.

Beyond visual and auditory data, AI and ML have the capacity to analyze genetic material. While the acquisition of eDNA samples remains a significant challenge, advancements in genomic sequencing coupled with AI-powered analysis tools are poised to revolutionize our understanding of the genetic landscape of the creature. AI algorithms can analyze DNA sequences with exceptional speed and accuracy, identifying potential matches within vast databases of known species. Moreover, AI can be used to predict the phenotypic characteristics of an organism based on its genetic makeup, providing insights into potential physical attributes of the creature based on scant genetic material. This approach avoids the subjectivity inherent in analyzing physical evidence, which has often been hampered by the lack of quality samples and questionable authentication.

The potential application of AI in predicting Bigfoot movements is another significant area of research. By combining various datasets including environmental factors (terrain, vegetation, water sources), weather patterns, and previously reported sightings, AI algorithms can build predictive models to anticipate Bigfoot activity. This could be particularly valuable for guiding field researchers to locations with a higher probability of encounters, optimizing limited resources, and maximizing the efficiency of fieldwork. This predictive capacity, however, is heavily dependent on the quality and quantity of the data used to train the models. Therefore, a concerted effort to collect and validate various datasets is essential before predictive modelling can reach its full potential.

However, the application of AI in Bigfoot research is not without its challenges. The accuracy and reliability of AI algorithms depend heavily on the quality and quantity of the training data. Given the scarcity of confirmed Bigfoot evidence, developing accurate and robust AI models poses a significant hurdle. Overfitting, a common problem in machine learning, where models perform well on training data but poorly on unseen data, is a real concern. Careful consideration needs to be given to the selection and curation of training data to ensure the validity of the results generated by AI algorithms. Careful cross-validation techniques must be employed to mitigate this risk and ensure the robustness of any inferences drawn from AI-generated outputs. Furthermore, the interpretation of the results requires a deep understanding of both the AI algorithms and the limitations of the data, preventing the over-reliance on potentially flawed predictions.

Another challenge involves the potential for biases in the training data. If the training datasets are biased toward certain interpretations or types of evidence, the resulting AI models might perpetuate and amplify these biases, leading to flawed conclusions. Researchers must ensure that the training data is diverse, representative, and free from inherent bias. Rigorous quality control measures should be in place to identify and mitigate the influence of human error or intentional manipulation in the dataset. The development of transparent and auditable AI models is essential to ensure the credibility and trust-worthiness of the research findings. Open-source algorithms and public access to the training datasets would further enhance the accountability and allow independent verification of the research process.

The ethical considerations surrounding the use of AI in Bigfoot research are also paramount. AI-driven technologies could be used for surveillance and tracking of Bigfoot, raising concerns about the potential violation of privacy and the disturbance of its natural habi-tat. Strict ethical guidelines must be established to ensure that any research involving AI respects the potential rights of Bigfoot as a sentient being, should its existence be confirmed. The responsible use of AI in Bigfoot research must consider not just scientific advancement but also the potential impact on the environment and the ethical treatment of wildlife, regardless of the entity's species clas-sification.

In summary, AI and machine learning offer powerful tools to advance Bigfoot research, enabling the objective analysis of vast datasets and the identification of patterns that may remain unde-tected by human researchers. However, the responsible development and application of these technologies requires careful consideration of potential biases, ethical implications, and the limitations of the available data. Addressing these challenges requires collaboration among researchers across various disciplines – computer scientists, biologists, zoologists, and ethicists – to ensure that the integration of AI in Bigfoot research is both scientifically rigorous and ethically sound. The future of Bigfoot research undoubtedly lies in the conflu-ence of innovative technology and responsible scientific practice. Only through this synergistic approach can we move beyond specula-tion and conjecture towards a more informed and objective under-standing of this enduring mystery. The integration of AI holds the potential for not only uncovering more evidence, but also fostering a more nuanced and ethical approach to the field of cryptozoology. It may ultimately lead to a deeper understanding of our planet's biodi-

versity and a more respectful approach to the study of elusive creatures. The journey may be long and complex, but the potential
rewards of utilizing AI in Bigfoot research are significant, offering a
tantalizing glimpse into a future where the pursuit of scientific truth
is aided by technological advancements.

36

CITIZEN SCIENCE AND CROWDSOURCING IN BIGFOOT RESEARCH

The integration of AI, while promising, only scratches the surface of the technological revolution impacting Bigfoot research. A crucial and complementary approach lies in harnessing the power of the public: citizen science and crowdsourcing. These methods leverage the collective efforts of numerous individuals, often amateur enthusiasts, to contribute data and analysis to scientific investigations. In the case of Bigfoot, the vastness of the potential search area, coupled with the creature's elusiveness, makes citizen involvement practically indispensable. While professional researchers have limited resources and time, a widespread network of dedicated individuals can cover significantly more ground, report more sightings, and collect a broader range of potential evidence.

One of the most successful examples of citizen science in related fields is the use of bird watching apps and online platforms that track bird migrations and populations. Millions of participants upload photos and location data, allowing researchers to monitor species distribution and population trends with unprecedented accuracy. A similar approach could revolutionize Bigfoot research. Imagine an app designed to record and geo-tag potential Bigfoot sightings, complete with timestamped photos, audio recordings of suspected vocalizations, and detailed descriptions of tracks or other physical evidence. This app could be designed with sophisticated filters and verification systems to help weed out false positives and ensure data quality.

The data generated by such an app could be exponentially larger than anything currently available to researchers. This wealth of information would require sophisticated algorithms and AI tools for effective analysis. However, the data itself, even in its raw, unprocessed form, represents a significant advancement. For example, the sheer number of reported sightings, even if many are ultimately attributed to misidentifications, could reveal geographical hotspots or patterns of activity. The accumulation of consistent reports from multiple independent sources in a specific region would lend greater weight to the credibility of a particular sighting than a lone, unverified claim.

Crowdsourcing can also be invaluable in analyzing existing data. Projects like the Zooniverse platform demonstrate the power of crowdsourcing for image analysis. Volunteers can be trained to identify specific features in images or videos, such as gait patterns, body morphology, or unusual characteristics of tracks. For example, a large number of volunteers could help sift through thousands of blurry photographs or video clips, identifying those with the highest likelihood of depicting a Bigfoot-like creature. This would significantly reduce the workload on professional researchers, allowing them to focus on the most promising leads. The collective human brainpower, even with varying levels of expertise, could prove invaluable in identifying subtle patterns or details that might escape the notice of AI algorithms.

However, the successful implementation of citizen science and crowdsourcing in Bigfoot research requires careful planning and execution. Several critical factors need to be addressed:

- **Data Verification and Quality Control:** A robust system is needed to filter out unreliable or inaccurate data. This could involve incorporating multiple levels of verification, such as requiring multiple independent reports for a given sighting, employing image analysis tools to check for evidence of manipulation, and implementing a peer-review system for submitted evidence.

- **Data Privacy and Ethical Considerations:** Collecting and using personal data from participants requires careful attention to ethical guidelines and data privacy regulations. Clear and transparent policies must be established to ensure the responsible handling of participant information.
- **Training and Education:** Participants need proper training and education on data collection methods, identification of potential misidentifications, and ethical considerations. This could involve online tutorials, workshops, or field training programs.
- **Incentives and Motivation:** Motivating volunteers to participate requires a variety of incentives, such as recognition for contributions, opportunities for collaborative research, and access to exclusive data and findings.
- **Collaboration and Communication:** Effective communication between researchers and citizen scientists is crucial for fostering trust, promoting participation, and ensuring data quality. This could involve creating online forums, organizing regular meetups, or developing communication channels for feedback and collaboration.

Successfully navigating these challenges is crucial. Poorly managed citizen science initiatives can generate more noise than signal, overwhelming researchers with unreliable data and under-mining the credibility of the entire endeavor. Therefore, careful planning, robust quality control mechanisms, and transparent communication are crucial for the success of this approach.

The integration of citizen science and crowdsourcing represents a paradigm shift in Bigfoot research. It moves away from the tradition-ally solitary, resource-constrained efforts of a few dedicated researchers to a more collaborative and inclusive approach. This approach leverages the collective power of the public, transforming the hunt for Bigfoot into a large-scale, community-driven scientific project. It's not simply about finding more evidence, although that is a significant potential outcome; it's about building a more robust, reliable, and credible body of knowledge. The challenges are considerable, but the potential rewards — a more comprehensive understanding of this enduring enigma and a wider public engagement with the scientific process — are undeniable. The future of Bigfoot research may well depend on the successful integration of these collective efforts. The potential for discovery, coupled with the enhanced scientific rigor that this approach allows, holds the key to unlocking the secrets of this elusive creature, perhaps finally shifting the conversation from speculation to credible scientific investigation. The democratization of research, facilitated by citizen science and crowdsourcing, not only expands the data collection capacity but also fosters a sense of shared ownership and accountability, essential ingredients for moving the field forward in a positive and credible manner. The potential impact extends beyond simply solving the Bigfoot mystery; it could provide a blueprint for future collaborative research in other areas of cryptozoology and, more broadly, in scientific exploration.

Furthermore, engaging the public in this way can foster a greater appreciation for biodiversity and wildlife conservation, shifting the focus from simply the hunt for Bigfoot to a broader appreciation of the natural world and the importance of protecting it. By incorporating ethical considerations and rigorous data verification methods, citizen science can contribute significantly to a more responsible and informed approach to investigating elusive species. The successful implementation of these tools requires not only technological innovation, but also a carefully constructed framework of collaboration, communication, and education. By working together, professional researchers and citizen scientists can unlock the immense potential of this collaborative approach, pushing the boundaries of Bigfoot research and possibly uncovering valuable insights into this enduring mystery. This collaborative approach can transform Bigfoot research from a fringe pursuit into a more rigorous and credible scientific endeavor. The blend of technological advancement with citizen engagement stands poised to revolutionize how we approach the enigma of Bigfoot, potentially bridging the gap between speculation and concrete evidence, and ultimately, answering one of nature's most enduring mysteries. The success of this approach depends on creating a strong, collaborative, and transparent system that prioritizes both data integrity and public engagement.

37

POTENTIAL HABITATS AND GEOGRAPHIC DISTRIBUTION OF BIGFOOT

The question of where Bigfoot might live, and how widespread its population might be, is central to any serious investigation. While definitive answers remain elusive, analyzing reported sightings, considering the creature's presumed ecological needs, and examining the environmental factors conducive to its survival allows us to construct a plausible picture of potential habitats and geographic distribution.

The overwhelming majority of reported Bigfoot sightings cluster in heavily forested regions of North America, specifically the Pacific Northwest and the mountainous areas of the western United States and Canada. This isn't surprising, given the creature's alleged size and presumed need for extensive, undisturbed wilderness. Dense coniferous forests, offering ample cover and abundant food sources, seem to be favored locations. The terrain is often rugged and mountainous, presenting challenges for human access, which might explain why Bigfoot sightings are less frequent in easily accessible areas. The mountainous regions of Washington, Oregon, California, Idaho, Montana, British Columbia, and Alberta consistently generate a high number of reported encounters.

However, this geographic concentration doesn't necessarily indicate that Bigfoot is confined to these areas. Reports, though less frequent, do emerge from other locations, including parts of the Appalachian Mountains, the Canadian Rockies, and even more isolated regions of Alaska. The sparse nature of these reports might be due to various factors: less human activity in these regions, resulting in fewer potential eyewitnesses; the inherent difficulty of traversing these remote areas, hindering investigations; or a genuine difference in population density. The possibility of isolated populations scattered across broader swathes of North America cannot be dismissed outright.

Understanding potential Bigfoot habitat requires examining the ecological requirements of a large, primate-like creature. Based on the descriptions of size and purported footprints, we can infer the need for substantial food sources. Researchers speculate a diet rich in vegetation, possibly including roots, berries, nuts, and other forest products. The presence of these food sources, combined with access to water sources like rivers and streams, becomes a crucial factor in defining potential Bigfoot habitat. The proximity of dense forest cover for protection from predators and the elements also significantly influences habitat suitability. The creatures would likely avoid areas of significant human activity, favoring zones with a lower human population density and minimal disturbance.

The environmental conditions play a critical role in shaping Bigfoot's potential range. The creature's purported aversion to extreme temperatures might restrict its distribution. While the creature's tolerance to cold climates is suggested by sightings in colder mountainous regions, areas with extreme winters or scorching summers could prove less hospitable. The availability of suitable food sources throughout the year would also be a significant factor limiting its range. Regions experiencing distinct seasons, with variation in food availability, might force the creature to migrate, further restricting its range or leading to localized population concentrations.

Furthermore, the quality of the forest itself is a significant factor. Old-growth forests, with their complex ecosystems and abundance of food sources, would likely be preferred over younger, less diverse forests. The presence of dense undergrowth offers both protection and ample foraging opportunities. Open areas, while potentially offering clear views for hunting and avoiding predators, would not offer adequate cover for a creature of Bigfoot's size and would thus likely be less frequented. This preference for mature forests, with their inherent complexity and cover, might contribute to the difficulty of finding evidence, making detection challenging even in seemingly appropriate areas.

Beyond the immediate ecological needs, the presence of human settlements and activity significantly impacts the potential habitat of Bigfoot. Reports suggest a strong correlation between reported sightings and areas with low human population density. Road construction, logging, and other forms of human development can fragment habitats, potentially isolating populations and making them more vulnerable. Habitat fragmentation could explain the sporadic nature of sightings across broader geographical zones, with isolated pockets of population surviving in undisturbed areas amidst human-altered landscapes.

The impact of human encroachment extends beyond simply reducing habitat size. Human disturbance, such as noise and light pollution, could significantly alter the behavior of Bigfoot, making it more elusive and difficult to observe. The potential for conflict between humans and Bigfoot, even if accidental, cannot be disregarded, adding further complexity to the issue of geographic distribution and habitat suitability.

In examining the potential geographic distribution of Bigfoot, it's crucial to consider the reliability and biases in reported sightings. Not all sightings are equally credible. Some could be misidentifications of known animals, while others might be the result of hoaxes or misinterpretations.

Analyzing the details of each report, considering the expertise and credibility of the witness, the environmental context, and any accompanying physical evidence, is crucial in developing a realistic picture. The inconsistencies in reports across various regions also need careful consideration, as these discrepancies could reflect genuine variations in population density, habitat suitability, or simply limitations in data collection.

Furthermore, the lack of concrete scientific evidence, such as DNA samples or conclusive physical remains, hinders a precise assessment of Bigfoot's geographic range. Existing research primarily relies on anecdotal evidence, footprint casts, and occasional visual sightings, each prone to interpretation and potential biases. Improving data collection methods, employing advanced technologies, and applying rigorous scientific methodology are crucial steps in developing a more accurate understanding of Bigfoot's potential habitat and its distribution across North America. The task, therefore, is not merely to map reported sightings, but to integrate this information with ecological knowledge, rigorous analysis, and a critical assessment of evidence to build a more robust and comprehensive model of potential Bigfoot habitats and their geographical reach. The continuing challenge lies in bridging the gap between anecdotal evidence and scientific validation, a challenge that demands innovative approaches and persistent investigation.

38

SOCIAL STRUCTURES, DIET, AND ACTIVITY PATTERNS

I nferring the behavior of a creature as elusive as Bigfoot presents a significant challenge. The lack of direct observation and controlled study necessitates reliance on indirect evidence, primarily eyewitness accounts, footprint analysis, and circumstantial findings. While each piece of evidence is individually susceptible to interpretation and potential biases, a collective examination can provide insights into potential behavioral patterns. Analyzing the distribution of reported sightings, for example, might hint at migratory patterns or seasonal movements linked to food availability or breeding cycles. Similarly, the size and depth of footprints, as well as their spacing, may suggest locomotion styles, gait, and even group dynamics. The types of vegetation found near reported sightings could potentially offer clues to dietary habits. The nature of any reported damage to the environment—broken branches, disturbed undergrowth—could reveal clues about their interactions with their surroundings. However, the inherent limitations of this indirect methodology require cautious interpretation, and any conclusions drawn must remain tentative until corroborated by more robust evidence. The key is to integrate various data points, considering potential biases and uncertainties, to build a comprehensive picture, rather than drawing definitive conclusions from individual observations.

The available evidence, though fragmented, suggests a degree of social structure amongst Bigfoot populations. Multiple sightings in close proximity, particularly reports of groups of individuals, hint at family units or small social groups. Some researchers propose a hierarchical structure, perhaps akin to other primates, with dominant individuals leading smaller groups. This hypothesis, however, requires substantial further investigation, as the evidence is currently insufficient to support definitive conclusions. The size and composition of these potential social groups remain unknown, ranging from solitary individuals to small family units or larger, more complex social structures. Further complicating the matter is the limited understanding of Bigfoot's reproductive strategies and life cycle. The frequency of reported sightings might offer hints, potentially suggesting peak activity during specific seasons or life stages. For instance, a heightened number of sightings during a certain time of year could correlate with breeding season, migration, or seasonal shifts in food availability. However, seasonal variations in human activity and reporting biases need to be carefully considered when interpreting such trends.

Analyzing reported encounters suggests potential dietary preferences, although the limitations of the available data make any definitive conclusions challenging. Many reported sightings occur near bodies of water or in areas rich in vegetation, suggesting a preference for riparian habitats and possibly a diet including plants, berries, and other vegetation. However, other accounts suggest instances of potential scavenging or predation, pointing to a more opportunistic diet. The alleged destruction of campsites and evidence of foraging behavior also suggest a varied diet and adaptive foraging strategies. Understanding the full extent of their diet is crucial for assessing their ecological role and potential impact on their habitat. Is Bigfoot primarily herbivorous, omnivorous, or even carnivorous? Further investigation utilizing DNA analysis of scat samples, if any are reliably sourced, could help elucidate their dietary preferences and nutritional needs.

The activity patterns of Bigfoot appear to be largely nocturnal or crepuscular, with most sightings reported during the early morning or late evening hours. This behavior might be an adaptation to avoid human encounters and maximize foraging efficiency. While some daytime sightings have been reported, these are considerably less frequent, possibly indicating a shift in activity patterns due to factors such as reduced human activity in certain areas or changing environmental conditions. Further complicating this, human activity itself can impact the observed activity patterns. If Bigfoot displays avoidance behavior, areas with high human presence may result in decreased daytime sightings. Conversely, in more remote areas with minimal human interference, sightings might occur more frequently, regardless of the time of day.

The existing data on Bigfoot activity patterns also needs careful consideration of reporting biases. It is reasonable to assume that nocturnal or crepuscular activity would make sightings more difficult, leading to underreporting compared to daytime activity. Additionally, certain environmental conditions, such as weather patterns or visibility, might impact the likelihood of an encounter and subsequent reporting. The impact of weather patterns on Bigfoot sightings and behavior remains an interesting but largely unexplored area of research. The effect of seasonal changes on their behavior, particularly relating to food availability and breeding cycles, should be more thoroughly studied. For instance, evidence of seasonal migration could provide valuable insight into their home ranges and spatial dynamics. Understanding these seasonal variations could lead to better strategies for locating and observing the creatures.

Footprint analysis provides a unique window into Bigfoot locomotion and potentially group dynamics. The size and depth of the footprints, coupled with their spacing, can provide clues about gait, size, and potentially even the number of individuals involved. However, the reliability of footprint evidence is often debated. The possibility of misidentification, hoaxing, or natural phenomena mimicking Bigfoot footprints cannot be dismissed. Rigorous scientific methods, including careful documentation, casting techniques, and comparative analysis, are crucial to assessing the validity of such evidence. Moreover, the geographic distribution of footprints, when reliably documented, might reveal information about potential migratory routes or preferred habitats.

The analysis of potential Bigfoot habitats reveals preferences for rugged, remote terrains with dense vegetation. Areas with readily available water sources, such as rivers, streams, and lakes, seem to be preferred. This observation aligns with the creature's presumed dietary and lifestyle needs, suggesting a preference for environments that offer both food and shelter. However, generalizations about habitat preferences should be approached with caution. While certain ecological factors might appear conducive to Bigfoot survival, other crucial aspects, such as social dynamics or predator-prey relationships, remain largely unknown. The correlation between reported sightings and environmental variables, such as vegetation density, altitude, and proximity to water sources, requires statistical analysis to eliminate biases and identify significant relationships. Such analysis, complemented by habitat suitability modeling, can refine our understanding of potential Bigfoot distribution and inform future search efforts.

Another crucial aspect in understanding Bigfoot behavior is analyzing its interaction with its environment. Reports of damaged trees, disturbed undergrowth, and potential signs of nest building provide some insight into their interaction with their habitat. However, interpreting such evidence requires caution. Other animals can cause similar damage, making it critical to eliminate alternative explanations. A multidisciplinary approach is essential here, integrating ecological expertise with forensic analysis to distinguish Bigfoot-related environmental changes from those attributable to other causes. Analyzing the types of vegetation found near reported sightings, coupled with scat analysis (if available), provides more detailed insight into their diet and nutritional requirements.

The impact of Bigfoot on its environment, if present, remains largely unknown. Their potential role in seed dispersal, nutrient cycling, or trophic cascades warrants investigation. Hypothetically, a large, possibly omnivorous creature could exert significant influence on the ecological balance of its habitat. However, without concrete evidence of its presence, assessing its ecological impact remains speculative. Further research might involve analyzing changes in vegetation patterns, soil composition, or animal populations in areas with frequent Bigfoot sightings. A comparative analysis of similar environments with and without reported Bigfoot activity might help reveal subtle, yet meaningful, ecological differences.

In conclusion, piecing together Bigfoot's behavioral patterns from fragmented evidence requires a meticulous and multifaceted approach. Integrating various data points, while carefully considering potential biases and limitations, is paramount. The current body of evidence, though inconclusive, hints at a complex creature with possible social structures, diverse dietary preferences, and largely nocturnal activity patterns. Future research should leverage advanced technologies, such as remote camera traps, DNA analysis, and improved data collection methods, to gather more robust and reliable evidence. Until then, any conclusions drawn remain speculative, demanding further investigation to unravel the mysteries surrounding Bigfoot's behavior and its impact on its environment. The journey continues, fueled by persistence and the pursuit of scientific rigor in the face of an enduring enigma.

39

IMPACT OF HUMAN ACTIVITY ON BIGFOOT POPULATIONS

The elusive nature of Bigfoot makes assessing the impact of human activity on its potential populations a particularly challenging endeavor. Lacking direct observational data, we must rely on indirect indicators, extrapolating from habitat destruction, encroachment, and the general effects of human presence on wildlife. The sheer scale of human influence on the environment, however, makes disentangling specific impacts on a creature as rare (and perhaps mythologized) as Bigfoot a complex task.

One of the most significant threats is habitat loss and fragmentation. Bigfoot, if it exists, is believed to inhabit remote, forested regions characterized by dense undergrowth and diverse ecosystems. The relentless expansion of human settlements, logging operations, and infrastructure development directly reduces the amount of suitable habitat available. Roads, pipelines, and power lines fragment these habitats, isolating populations and limiting access to vital resources like food and mates. This fragmentation can lead to inbreeding, reduced genetic diversity, and increased vulnerability to disease, all of which can negatively affect population viability. The specific impact on a species like Bigfoot, whose population size and distribution are unknown, is purely speculative, but the principle holds true across many species. The loss of old-growth forests, in particular, is devastating, as these ancient ecosystems provide crucial cover and a wide array of food sources. Their destruction disrupts established ecological balances, potentially removing critical resources Bigfoot might rely on.

Mining activities pose another significant threat. The disturbance of the land, noise pollution, and heavy machinery disrupt the delicate balance of the ecosystem, forcing wildlife to flee or adapt to increasingly hostile environments. The resulting habitat alteration can lead to displacement, reduced food availability, and increased stress levels. This is exacerbated in areas where mining activities are coupled with deforestation, effectively creating a double whammy of environmental damage. Furthermore, the introduction of heavy metals and other pollutants into the soil and water can have long-term consequences for the health of the ecosystem and any creatures inhabiting it, potentially leading to bioaccumulation of toxins within the food chain. This is a concern not just for potential Bigfoot populations but for the entire biodiversity of the affected areas.

Similarly, the expansion of agriculture and livestock grazing also dramatically alters the landscape. Large-scale farming practices often lead to deforestation and the conversion of natural habitats into monoculture landscapes, offering little in the way of sustenance or cover for a creature such as Bigfoot. The use of pesticides and herbicides can also contaminate the environment, potentially impacting the health and survival of any wildlife inhabiting the area. The noise and human activity associated with these operations further contribute to habitat disturbance, potentially forcing Bigfoot into increasingly marginal areas.

Human encroachment also leads to increased encounters between humans and Bigfoot, potentially resulting in conflict. As human populations expand into traditionally remote areas, the chances of accidental encounters increase. This increased human presence can disrupt Bigfoot's behavioral patterns, leading to increased stress, altered foraging behaviors, and potentially even confrontations. Fear of human contact could lead to behavioral changes that negatively affect the population's ability to thrive. While direct conflict is a remote possibility, the stress caused by increased human activity is a likely contributor to potential population decline.

The impact of climate change further complicates the picture. Changes in temperature and precipitation patterns can drastically alter the distribution and abundance of plants and animals within an ecosystem, potentially impacting the food sources available to Bigfoot. Extreme weather events, such as droughts, floods, and wildfires, can further damage habitats, making them unsuitable for wildlife. The indirect consequences of climate change, such as changes in the distribution of insect populations, which could significantly impact the food chain, could also have far-reaching effects. The interconnectedness of ecological systems means that even seemingly minor changes can have cascading effects throughout the entire food web, making accurate prediction of the specific impacts on Bigfoot extremely challenging.

Another less obvious, yet potentially significant, impact is light pollution. Nocturnal animals like Bigfoot (if its nocturnal habits are indeed confirmed), are especially vulnerable to the effects of artificial light. Light pollution can disrupt their natural behaviors, affecting their ability to forage, navigate, and reproduce. It can also make them more vulnerable to predation or human encounters. The constant illumination of night landscapes disrupts natural circadian rhythms, affecting various physiological processes. Longterm exposure to artificial light at night has been linked to numerous negative impacts on wildlife, from reduced reproductive success to increased susceptibility to disease.

Finally, recreational activities, including off-road vehicle use and hiking, can also disrupt Bigfoot habitats. The noise and disturbance caused by these activities can scare wildlife away, fragment habitats, and leave behind trails of litter and other pollutants. Off-road vehicles, in particular, are known to cause significant habitat damage and soil erosion, negatively impacting the overall health of the ecosystem. The cumulative effect of these recreational pressures, even if individually small, can have a considerable impact on vulnerable populations.

Quantifying the precise impact of human activities on Bigfoot populations remains incredibly difficult, primarily due to the lack of direct evidence regarding Bigfoot's existence and its population dynamics. However, by examining the broader impacts of habitat destruction, encroachment, and environmental degradation on similar species, we can extrapolate some potential consequences. The fact that Bigfoot is believed to inhabit remote wilderness areas puts it at considerable risk from human expansion. Any efforts to protect the potential habitat of this creature necessarily needs to focus on broader conservation initiatives aimed at preserving biodiversity and protecting endangered species. Until concrete evidence of Bigfoot's existence is found, however, we can only rely on indirect measures and inferences to gauge the potential impact of human activities. The focus, therefore, should remain on the preservation of pristine wilderness areas, regardless of the presence or absence of Bigfoot. The long-term health of these ecosystems, and the countless species that call them home, is paramount. Preservation of these habitats benefits not only potential Bigfoot populations but all wildlife, and maintains the overall balance of our planet's ecosystems. The ongoing debate surrounding Bigfoot's existence should not overshadow the critical need for environmental conservation.

40

PROTECTING BIGFOOT AND ITS HABITAT

The inherent challenges in addressing Bigfoot's conservation needs stem directly from the creature's elusive nature. We lack concrete evidence of its existence, population size, or precise habitat requirements. This absence of data significantly hinders any targeted conservation efforts. Instead of focusing on a hypothetical Bigfoot-specific conservation plan, a more pragmatic approach centers on protecting the vast wilderness areas where Bigfoot is *allegedly* found. This strategy aligns perfectly with broader conservation goals, benefiting countless other species while indirectly safeguarding any potential Bigfoot populations. The preservation of these ecosystems is crucial regardless of the existence of Bigfoot, as these areas are vital biodiversity hotspots often harboring endangered or threatened plants and animals.

The crucial point is that protecting potential Bigfoot habitat is intrinsically linked to protecting entire ecosystems. Focusing solely on Bigfoot risks diverting resources from proven conservation efforts that address the immediate needs of known endangered species. The resources – both financial and human – dedicated to confirming or denying Bigfoot's existence could be redirected toward more tangible conservation goals. Furthermore, the intense media attention surrounding Bigfoot can inadvertently lead to increased human traffic in sensitive ecosystems, thus undermining conservation efforts targeting established wildlife. Uncontrolled human access can disturb wildlife, damage fragile habitats, and introduce invasive species, ultimately harming biodiversity.

Consider the Pacific Northwest, a region frequently associated with Bigfoot sightings. This area boasts a rich tapestry of biodiversity, including old-growth forests, critical salmon spawning grounds, and diverse wildlife populations. Threats to this region include logging, mining, and urban sprawl. Protecting this habitat isn't solely about Bigfoot; it's about preserving a vital ecosystem that sustains countless species, many of which are already classified as threatened or endangered. The conservation efforts in this region should prioritize preserving the existing ecosystem's integrity, which would indirectly benefit any potential Bigfoot populations.

One could argue that the very uncertainty surrounding Bigfoot's existence strengthens the case for broad-based conservation. The unknown factor should act as a catalyst, emphasizing the need for precautionary measures. If Bigfoot does exist, and if its habitat is compromised, the consequences could be severe, not only for the creature itself but also for the overall ecological balance. The precautionary principle, widely used in environmental policy, suggests that when there is uncertainty about the potential impacts of a human activity, action should err on the side of caution. In the context of Bigfoot and its potential habitat, this means that we should prioritize the protection of wilderness areas, regardless of whether Bigfoot exists, to mitigate any potential harm.

This approach necessitates a shift in perspective. Instead of prioritizing the search for Bigfoot itself, the focus must be on comprehensive ecosystem management. This includes sustainable forestry practices, responsible mining operations, the establishment of protected areas, and public education initiatives that promote environmental stewardship. These measures not only safeguard the potential habitat of Bigfoot but also address critical environmental concerns, such as climate change, habitat loss, and biodiversity decline.

Furthermore, the potential impact of human activity on Bigfoot, should it exist, extends beyond habitat destruction. Noise pollution from human activities, such as logging, mining, and recreational activities, could disrupt Bigfoot's behavior and communication patterns. Light pollution, particularly from expanding urban areas, could similarly disrupt its nocturnal habits. The introduction of invasive species could also alter the delicate balance of the ecosystem, potentially affecting Bigfoot's food sources or exposing it to new diseases. These indirect impacts emphasize the importance of minimizing human disturbance within potential Bigfoot habitat.

The challenge, therefore, isn't just about finding Bigfoot but understanding and protecting the intricate web of life that sustains it, assuming it exists. Investing in research focused on understanding the ecological dynamics of these wilderness areas is far more valuable than solely searching for the creature. This research could yield invaluable information about the overall health of these ecosystems, allowing for more effective conservation strategies. The knowledge gained would benefit numerous species and, incidentally, any potential Bigfoot populations as well.

While the debate surrounding Bigfoot's existence continues, the need for responsible environmental stewardship remains paramount. The pursuit of this elusive creature should not overshadow the critical need for proactive conservation efforts. Instead, the uncertainty surrounding Bigfoot should serve as a reminder of the vast unknowns within our ecosystems and the importance of preserving them for the benefit of all species, known and unknown.

The conservation of potential Bigfoot habitat needs to be integrated into larger-scale regional and national conservation plans. Collaboration between government agencies, non-profit organizations, and indigenous communities with traditional knowledge of the land is crucial for effective conservation management. Indigenous communities often possess invaluable insights into the local ecosystems and their inhabitants, information that can inform and enhance conservation efforts. Their perspectives and knowledge should be actively sought and incorporated into any conservation strategies.

The ethical implications of Bigfoot research also deserve careful consideration. Any research activities should be conducted in a manner that minimizes disturbance to the ecosystem and avoids any potential harm to wildlife. Respect for the environment and its inhabitants should guide all research efforts. The emphasis should always be on minimizing the impact of human activities, rather than maximizing the chances of a Bigfoot sighting.

Ultimately, the question of Bigfoot's conservation is inextricably linked to the broader issue of wilderness preservation. By focusing on the preservation of the vast and pristine wilderness areas where Bigfoot is reportedly found, we simultaneously protect a multitude of species and ecosystems. This holistic approach not only addresses the potential needs of Bigfoot, but also safeguards the health and integrity of our planet's biodiversity for generations to come. The pursuit of the unknown should not come at the expense of the known, and the preservation of these ecosystems, regardless of Bigfoot's existence, is of paramount importance. The long-term health and stability of these wild spaces far outweigh the short-term appeal of solving the Bigfoot mystery. The focus must remain on preserving the biodiversity of these ecosystems for the benefit of all life within them. The enigmatic presence of Bigfoot, whether real or imagined, should serve as a reminder of the vast and largely unknown wonders that still exist within our world, and the urgency with which we must protect them.

41

POTENTIAL IMPACTS AND ADAPTATIONS

The previous discussion highlighted the inherent difficulties in formulating specific conservation strategies for Bigfoot due to the lack of concrete evidence regarding its existence, population size, and habitat preferences. However, if we assume, for the sake of this analysis, that Bigfoot does exist, it becomes crucial to consider the potential impacts of climate change on its survival and the adaptive strategies it might employ. The very ecosystems believed to harbor this elusive creature are undergoing dramatic transformations, and understanding these changes is essential to assessing its potential vulnerability.

Climate change presents a multifaceted threat to Bigfoot, assuming its existence. The most immediate danger likely stems from habitat loss and fragmentation. Bigfoot is reportedly found in remote, forested areas characterized by dense vegetation and ample water sources. Rising global temperatures, increased frequency and intensity of wildfires, and changes in precipitation patterns are all contributing to the degradation and shrinking of these crucial habitats. The encroachment of human development, often driven by population growth and resource extraction, further exacerbates this issue, creating a double whammy of habitat destruction and fragmentation.

Increased temperatures could also directly impact Bigfoot's physiology and behavior. Depending on its physiological adaptations, Bigfoot might struggle to regulate its body temperature in increasingly warmer climates. This could lead to reduced foraging efficiency, increased stress, and ultimately, reduced reproductive success. Moreover, changing precipitation patterns could influence the availability of food sources, disrupting the creature's established foraging patterns. Reduced snowpack in mountainous regions, which are often cited as key Bigfoot habitats, could also affect access to water and food, impacting seasonal migrations or denning behaviors. The disruption of established seasonal patterns, a hallmark of climate change, could further exacerbate these difficulties.

However, the potential for Bigfoot to adapt to these changes cannot be dismissed. We have limited understanding of its physiological capabilities and behavioral flexibility. Over millennia, many species have demonstrated remarkable resilience in the face of environmental change, evolving strategies to cope with fluctuating conditions. Bigfoot, if it exists, might possess unanticipated adaptive mechanisms. These could include alterations in its foraging habits, shifts in its geographical range, or even changes in its physiology to better tolerate warmer temperatures.

The absence of concrete biological data necessitates a cautious approach. While we lack the detailed knowledge needed to predict Bigfoot's exact responses to climate change, the documented impact of such changes on other large mammals offers valuable insights. Similar large-bodied species in similar environments could serve as analogs, albeit imperfect ones. The impacts of climate change on bears, for example, provide a useful case study. Studies have documented shifts in bear behavior, including altered hibernation patterns and ranges, in response to climate driven changes in food availability and habitat suitability. These examples provide some insight into potential Bigfoot responses.

Another significant factor is the cascading effect of climate change on the ecosystem as a whole. The disruption of ecological balance, caused by climate change, doesn't just directly impact Bigfoot, but also the plants and animals that form its food web. If key plant species diminish or disappear due to temperature changes or altered precipitation, Bigfoot's dietary options might drastically change, forcing it to adapt or face starvation. Similarly, competition for resources with other species, also affected by climate change, could intensify, adding further pressure on any existing Bigfoot populations. A disruption to the overall ecological balance, perhaps even the disappearance of certain prey species, could trigger a domino effect that threatens Bigfoot's survival.

It is essential to emphasize the limitations of this analysis. The lack of direct observational data on Bigfoot hampers accurate prediction of its adaptive capacity. Our knowledge is fundamentally speculative, based on the characteristics of other large mammals in similar habitats and general principles of evolutionary biology and ecology. Yet, the potential vulnerability of any species to the impacts of climate change, regardless of its elusiveness, highlights the urgency of broader conservation strategies.

Protecting the large wilderness areas where Bigfoot is allegedly observed is not just about preserving a potential Bigfoot population; it's a fundamental conservation strategy that benefits countless other species. These areas act as carbon sinks, mitigating climate change itself. Their preservation also safeguards biodiversity hotspots, offering resilience against future environmental changes. Furthermore, protecting these wilderness areas provides opportunities for future research, not only on Bigfoot, but also on the broader impacts of climate change on ecosystems. Advanced technological approaches such as remote sensing, genetic analysis of environmental DNA (eDNA), and sophisticated camera trap systems could be employed in a comprehensive and scientific approach, even with the difficulties presented by the creature's elusiveness.

The future of Bigfoot, if it exists, is inextricably linked to the future of these wild ecosystems. Therefore, efforts toward mitigating climate change and preserving wilderness areas are crucial steps in ensuring its survival, regardless of the certainty surrounding its existence. Focusing on broader conservation strategies not only indirectly safeguards potential Bigfoot populations but also ensures the health and stability of the planet's biodiversity for generations to come. Investing in sustainable practices and promoting environmental consciousness transcends the specific mystery of Bigfoot, providing a framework for protecting countless other species, and potentially future discoveries.

The lack of conclusive evidence regarding Bigfoot's existence should not detract from the importance of understanding the potential impact of climate change on the ecosystems where it is *allegedly* found. The ongoing environmental crisis impacts all life on the planet, regardless of the presence or absence of a specific, yet-to-be-proven cryptid. The focus remains on preserving biodiversity, reducing greenhouse gas emissions, and adopting sustainable practices for the benefit of the entire planet. The mystery of Bigfoot, in this context, serves as a compelling reminder of the unexplored and often unknown wonders of the natural world that urgently require our protection. Furthermore, the search for Bigfoot and the study of its purported habitat provides a unique opportunity to engage the public in broader environmental issues and conservation efforts. The fascination surrounding the mystery fuels a dialogue about preserving wilderness areas, a crucial aspect of both climate change mitigation and overall biodiversity protection.

The ongoing research Into climate change effects on various species offers a crucial framework for understanding the potential impact on Bigfoot, even in the absence of concrete proof of its existence. The lessons learned from studying other large mammals, and indeed the entire ecosystem, within its potential range, can be extrapolated and applied to better understand the challenges this cryptid might face. It is important to emphasize the need for responsible research methodologies; however, this should not overshadow the critical need for proactive environmental protection. Even if Bigfoot remains unproven, protecting its alleged habitat safeguards countless other species and vital ecosystems.

In conclusion, while the potential impacts of climate change on Bigfoot remain speculative, they underscore the vital importance of protecting the vast wilderness areas where it is believed to reside. The conservation of these ecosystems transcends the specific mystery of Bigfoot, benefitting countless other species and playing a critical role in mitigating the effects of climate change. This holistic approach, emphasizing the preservation of biodiversity and sustainable practices, is far more impactful and enduring than any narrowly focused effort to solve the Bigfoot enigma. The pursuit of the unknown should never come at the expense of the known, and the preservation of these invaluable ecosystems remains paramount.

42

ACCESS TO PUBLIC LANDS AND RESEARCH PERMITS

The pursuit of Bigfoot, an endeavor often shrouded in mystery and fueled by passionate belief, is not exempt from the complexities of the law. Accessing the vast wilderness areas where sightings are most frequently reported necessitates navigating a labyrinthine system of regulations and permits. This section will examine the legal framework governing access to public lands crucial for Bigfoot research, highlighting the challenges and considerations for researchers operating within this framework.

The primary legal hurdle faced by Bigfoot researchers is access to public lands. Much of the terrain believed to be Bigfoot habitat falls under the jurisdiction of federal, state, or local governments. Federal lands, managed by agencies such as the Bureau of Land Management (BLM), the United States Forest Service (USFS), and the National Park Service (NPS), are subject to a range of regulations depending on the specific location and designated use. These regulations often dictate permissible activities, including research, camping, and off-road vehicle use. Unauthorized access can lead to fines and even criminal charges.

Obtaining permits for research on federal lands usually requires submitting a detailed research proposal outlining the study's objectives, methodology, and timeline. These proposals are subject to review by the managing agency to ensure that the proposed research is scientifically sound, environmentally responsible, and does not disrupt the natural environment or pose a threat to wildlife or public safety. The review process can be lengthy, often requiring several months or even years, and the outcome is not guaranteed. Factors considered during the review process often include the potential impact on wildlife, the preservation of sensitive ecosystems, and the researcher's qualifications and experience. Furthermore, certain areas within federal lands might be off-limits altogether due to environmental sensitivity, cultural significance, or ongoing conservation efforts, potentially restricting access to prime Bigfoot habitat.

State and local lands also present similar access challenges. State parks, wildlife refuges, and other protected areas typically have their own regulations regarding research activities. Researchers must familiarize themselves with these regulations and secure the necessary permits before embarking on their investigations. Obtaining these permits can involve navigating different bureaucratic processes, filling out extensive paperwork, and adhering to specific guidelines related to data collection, sample handling, and potential environmental impacts. The degree of scrutiny can vary depending on the specific location and the perceived risk associated with the proposed research. In some cases, local ordinances may place further restrictions on land access, adding another layer of complexity to the permitting process.

Beyond navigating the permit system, researchers must also adhere to relevant wildlife protection laws. Depending on the location, Bigfoot research could intersect with protections afforded to other species, whether threatened, endangered, or simply protected under state or federal wildlife regulations. For instance, if a researcher uses tracking methods that inadvertently disturb other wildlife, they could face penalties under existing conservation laws. The ethical dimension is crucial here: the pursuit of evidence relating to Bigfoot should not come at the expense of harming or disrupting other species inhabiting these delicate ecosystems.

Moreover, the handling and analysis of potential evidence, such as hair samples or footprints, are subject to stringent guidelines. Researchers must ensure that any collected material is properly documented, preserved, and analyzed in a way that minimizes contamination and maintains the integrity of the evidence. Failure to adhere to these guidelines could compromise the scientific value of the evidence and even lead to legal repercussions. Any violation of established protocols could render evidence inadmissible in a court of law or seriously undermine the credibility of the research itself.

The responsible use of research data also carries significant legal implications. Researchers must adhere to data privacy regulations, particularly when collecting or analyzing information that might inadvertently involve human subjects. Maintaining the confidentiality of landowners, witnesses, and other individuals involved in the research is paramount, and failure to do so could result in legal action. Clear guidelines on data sharing and collaboration among researchers are crucial to prevent breaches of privacy and ensure the ethical handling of sensitive information.

Beyond these routine challenges, Bigfoot research has occasionally led to legal disputes. Access to private land, for instance, requires explicit permission from landowners, and unauthorized entry constitutes trespassing, a serious offense. Disputes may arise over conflicting claims to evidence or allegations of damage to property during research activities. Navigating these legal complexities may require legal counsel specialized in land rights and environmental law, adding another layer of financial and logistical challenges to the already demanding field of Bigfoot investigation.

Looking towards the future, the development of clear regulations and guidelines specifically addressing Bigfoot research could streamline the permitting process, reduce the potential for conflicts, and help ensure that future investigations are conducted in a responsible and ethical manner. A collaborative effort involving researchers, government agencies, and legal experts could play a vital role in developing a cohesive framework that protects both the integrity of the research and the environment in which it is conducted. Such a framework could outline best practices for evidence collection, data management, and public outreach, fostering a more transparent and sustainable approach to Bigfoot research. In conclusion, while the pursuit of Bigfoot remains shrouded in mystery, the legal framework within which this pursuit takes place is far from ambiguous. Researchers must carefully navigate a complex web of regulations to ensure their investigations remain compliant with the law while adhering to ethical standards and the principles of scientific integrity. The future of Bigfoot research relies not only on technological advancements but also on a deeper understanding and compliance with the legal landscape within which the search takes place.

43

PROTECTION OF WILDLIFE AND ENDANGERED SPECIES LAWS

The complexities of Bigfoot research extend beyond navigating permit systems and land access regulations; they deeply intertwine with the overarching framework of wildlife protection and endangered species laws. While the very existence of *Sasquatch* remains unproven, the implications of assuming it exists, and operating under that assumption during research, have significant legal ramifications. The potential impact on existing wildlife populations and habitats, whether direct or indirect, cannot be ignored. The very act of pursuing Bigfoot, especially through intrusive methods, could inadvertently disrupt established ecosystems and endanger protected species. For example, researchers using drones for aerial surveillance might inadvertently disturb nesting birds or other sensitive wildlife, violating regulations aimed at preserving biodiversity. Similarly, the use of trail cameras, while seemingly innocuous, could lead to the unintended documentation of protected species, raising concerns about data privacy and potential misuse of such information.

The potential for unintended consequences extends beyond the immediate impact on wildlife. The public's fascination with Bigfoot attracts many individuals to areas already stressed by human activity, leading to increased pressure on fragile ecosystems. This influx of people could result in habitat degradation through trampling vegeta-tion, disturbing wildlife, littering, and potentially even poaching. Researchers themselves, despite their best intentions, can contribute to this problem if they fail to adhere strictly to responsible environ-mental practices. Therefore, any research project concerning Bigfoot must incorporate thorough environmental impact assessments and adhere to strict protocols to minimize disruption and potential harm.

Consider the Endangered Species Act (ESA) in the United States, a landmark piece of legislation designed to protect imperiled species and their habitats. Under the ESA, it is illegal to "take" a listed species, a term that encompasses a broad range of actions, including harassing, harming, pursuing, hunting, shooting, wounding, killing, trapping, capturing, or collecting. Even if Bigfoot were to be discov-ered and found to be a previously unknown species, the presump-tion of its protected status under the ESA—or equivalent legislation in other countries—would be likely. This automatically places significant constraints on any research involving direct interaction, trapping, or even close observation that could be considered harass-ment. Researchers would have to obtain extensive permits and demonstrate that any potential disturbance is minimal and justified by the scientific value of the research. This process is rigorous, and rightfully so, as the preservation of endangered species is paramount.

The legal landscape is not uniform across jurisdictions. Different countries and states have varying levels of protection for wildlife, and laws regulating research activities in wilderness areas can be complex and nuanced. For example, some areas may be designated as wildlife refuges or national parks with stricter access limitations and research protocols compared to less protected areas. Researchers must famil-iarize themselves thoroughly with the specific laws and regulations in effect for the location of their study, ensuring complete compliance. Furthermore, the use of any technology, such as remote sensing equipment or drones, may require additional permits and approvals from relevant regulatory bodies, such as the Federal Aviation Admin-istration (FAA) in the United States. Failure to do so can lead to serious legal consequences, including hefty fines and potential criminal charges.

Beyond the ESA and other specific wildlife protection acts, general environmental laws also play a significant role. These often cover aspects such as waste disposal, water pollution, and habitat destruction. Researchers venturing into remote areas must adhere to strict guidelines regarding waste management, ensuring that all materials, including trash and potentially even camera traps, are removed from the environment upon completion of field work. Leaving behind litter or equipment can not only harm wildlife, but also violate environmental laws with associated penalties. Equally important is considering the potential impact of any research activity on water resources. If researchers set up camp near a stream or river, they must follow strict guidelines to minimize the risk of water contamination through wastewater disposal or accidental spills of chemicals or fuels.

Furthermore, ethical considerations intertwined with the legal framework are essential for Bigfoot research. While the pursuit of scientific knowledge is critical, the potential impact on existing wildlife populations must be considered paramount. Research activities should be designed to minimize any potential harm, both direct and indirect, to the environment and its inhabitants. This requires careful planning, thorough risk assessments, and stringent adherence to responsible research practices. It necessitates a comprehensive understanding of the ecology of the area, the behavior of various species, and the sensitivity of their habitats. Researchers must actively seek to avoid disturbing animal behavior, breeding grounds, or other critical aspects of their life cycles.

The responsibility extends beyond merely complying with laws; researchers should be proactive in promoting conservation. This could include contributing to broader conservation efforts in the areas where they work, supporting local conservation organizations, and educating the public about environmental protection. Documenting any observed wildlife interactions, including those of protected species, should be done responsibly and with respect for their privacy and well-being. Any data collected should be handled according to ethical guidelines and relevant data protection regulations. Sharing data responsibly with relevant authorities might prove beneficial for ongoing conservation efforts.

The pursuit of Bigfoot, therefore, requires a nuanced understanding of the complex legal and ethical landscape governing wildlife protection. Researchers must not only obtain necessary permits and comply with environmental regulations, but also demonstrate a deep commitment to responsible research practices and environmental stewardship. Any potential discovery of Bigfoot would require a highly sensitive and collaborative approach involving multiple stakeholders, including government agencies, scientific communities, and local communities, to ensure both the creature's well-being and the preservation of its habitat. The future of Bigfoot research hinges not only on scientific breakthroughs but also on a profound commitment to ethical and legal responsibility. Ignoring these crucial aspects risks jeopardizing future investigations and potentially inflicting irreversible harm upon the environment and the very wildlife the research aims to understand. The quest for this enigmatic creature must be pursued with the utmost respect for the established legal and ethical framework governing the protection of wildlife and the natural world. Only through this responsible approach can the pursuit of knowledge coexist with the critical need for environmental protection. This balance is essential, not only for the integrity of Bigfoot research but for the well-being of our planet and all its inhabitants.

44

DATA PRIVACY AND THE RESPONSIBLE USE OF RESEARCH DATA

The ethical considerations surrounding data collection in Bigfoot research extend far beyond simply obtaining the necessary permits. The digital age has profoundly impacted how we gather and analyze information, introducing both unprecedented opportunities and significant challenges related to data privacy and responsible data usage. Researchers employing technological tools such as trail cameras, drones equipped with high-resolution cameras, thermal imaging devices, and even sophisticated acoustic monitoring systems generate vast amounts of data. This data often extends beyond the targeted subject of Bigfoot, encompassing images and recordings of other wildlife, potentially including endangered or protected species, as well as recordings capturing human activity on private or publicly protected lands. The responsible handling and usage of this data are therefore of paramount importance.

The question of data privacy becomes particularly acute when considering the potential for inadvertently capturing images or recordings of individuals without their consent. Trail cameras, for instance, often have wide fields of view, capturing not only the intended animal subjects but also hikers, campers, or even residents near the research area. The dissemination of such images or recordings, without informed consent, could lead to violations of privacy rights, potentially resulting in legal action. Similarly, the use of drones for aerial surveillance raises important questions about the right to privacy and potential intrusions into personal spaces. Strict adherence to relevant privacy regulations is therefore mandatory for all Bigfoot researchers.

Beyond individual privacy concerns, the data collected during Bigfoot research may also contain sensitive information about ecosystems and wildlife populations. This data, if improperly handled or shared, could be exploited for purposes unrelated to scientific research. For example, detailed information about the location of rare or endangered species could be misused by poachers or illegal wildlife traders, directly threatening the conservation efforts of those working to protect them. Furthermore, the location data associated with Bigfoot sightings, even if inconclusive, could trigger unwarranted human activity in sensitive habitats, leading to environmental degradation or disruption of the natural ecosystem.

The responsible use of research data necessitates the establishment of rigorous data management protocols. This includes implementing secure data storage systems, utilizing appropriate encryption techniques, and restricting access to sensitive data only to authorized researchers. Researchers should also establish clear guidelines regarding data sharing, ensuring that any collaboration or external dissemination of data adheres to ethical standards and relevant legal frameworks, including data protection laws like GDPR (General Data Protection Regulation) or CCPA (California Consumer Privacy Act) where applicable. Transparency and informed consent are crucial elements of responsible data usage. Researchers should clearly communicate to all stakeholders—landowners, government agencies, and the public—the purpose of their research, the methods they employ, and the potential implications of data collection.

The long-term storage and archiving of data pose additional considerations. Bigfoot research data, given the subject's elusive nature, might not yield immediate results. Researchers often accumulate large datasets over extended periods, requiring robust and sustainable storage solutions. The development of appropriate archiving strategies is necessary to preserve the integrity of the data and ensure its accessibility for future researchers, while simultaneously respecting privacy regulations and avoiding the potential for data corruption or loss. Furthermore, data preservation should be planned with sustainability in mind, ensuring that the data remains accessible and usable despite technological advancements and changes in storage formats.

Another significant aspect of responsible data usage is the proper attribution and citation of data sources. If researchers utilize data collected by others, they have a moral and legal obligation to acknowledge the original source and obtain permission if necessary. This not only upholds academic integrity but also respects the efforts and rights of other researchers. Failure to properly cite sources can lead to accusations of plagiarism and undermine the credibility of the research itself. Similarly, researchers should be transparent about any limitations or biases present in their data, acknowledging potential inaccuracies or uncertainties. This enhances the scientific rigor of the study and helps prevent misinterpretations of the results.

Furthermore, researchers need to establish clear protocols for handling data anomalies or unexpected findings. For example, if a trail camera captures images that seem to depict a creature consistent with descriptions of Bigfoot, researchers must carefully assess the evidence and avoid premature conclusions. It is crucial to analyze the image quality, eliminate potential alternative explanations (such as misidentifications or hoaxes), and determine the appropriate steps for sharing or publishing the findings. Premature dissemination of unsubstantiated claims could generate public misinformation and hinder future research efforts.

The issue of data ownership and intellectual property rights also needs careful consideration. While researchers might possess the data they collect, they need to be mindful of potential conflicts over ownership, particularly in cases involving publicly owned land or data obtained in collaboration with other institutions. Clear agreements and contractual arrangements are crucial to defining ownership, usage rights, and access restrictions for the collected data. The increasing reliance on digital technologies in Bigfoot research necessitates a proactive approach to addressing these legal and ethical aspects.

In conclusion, the ethical and legal considerations concerning data privacy and the responsible use of research data in the context of Bigfoot research are complex and multifaceted. Researchers have a significant responsibility to ensure that their data collection and management practices adhere to the highest ethical standards and legal requirements. By implementing robust data management protocols, emphasizing transparency, obtaining informed consent, and prioritizing data security and privacy, researchers can maintain the integrity of their work, protect the rights of others, and contribute to the responsible pursuit of knowledge concerning this elusive creature. The future of Bigfoot research depends not only on technological advancements but also on the unwavering commitment to responsible data handling. Negligence in this area can irrevocably damage the credibility of the field and jeopardize the delicate balance between scientific inquiry and environmental stewardship. Only through a robust ethical framework can the pursuit of this enduring mystery be conducted in a way that respects both the scientific method and our shared responsibility towards protecting the environment and safeguarding the rights of all individuals. The development of best practices, perhaps through the formation of a professional organization dedicated to Bigfoot research, could provide a crucial framework for ensuring ethical and responsible conduct within the field. Such an organization could develop and disseminate standardized guidelines for data collection, management, and sharing, establishing a baseline for responsible research that elevates the credibility and integrity of the field as a whole. The pursuit of knowledge should always be tempered by a commitment to ethical conduct, and in the realm of Bigfoot research, this commitment is especially crucial.

45

LEGAL CHALLENGES AND CASE STUDIES IN BIGFOOT RELATED DISPUTES

The ethical considerations discussed in the previous chapter naturally lead to a crucial aspect of Bigfoot research: the legal ramifications. The pursuit of this elusive creature often involves navigating complex legal landscapes, particularly concerning land access and the potential for disputes arising from research activities. While the excitement of a potential Bigfoot sighting can be overwhelming, researchers must operate within the bounds of the law, respecting property rights and adhering to regulations governing wildlife observation and data collection. Failure to do so can lead to significant legal challenges, ranging from trespassing charges to more serious offenses, depending on the specific circumstances and the jurisdiction involved.

One of the most frequent legal challenges faced by Bigfoot researchers involves land access. Much of the habitat believed to be suitable for Bigfoot—remote wilderness areas, national forests, and private property—requires permission to enter. Unauthorized access is a clear violation of the law and can result in fines, arrest, and even civil lawsuits from landowners. Researchers must diligently obtain the necessary permits and permissions before conducting any fieldwork on public or private land. This process often involves navigating bureaucratic procedures, contacting multiple agencies, and demonstrating a legitimate research purpose. The complexity of this process can be a significant barrier to entry for many researchers, particularly those operating on limited budgets or lacking experience in navigating legal frameworks.

Case studies illustrate the potential for conflict. In one instance, a team of researchers attempting to set up trail cameras on a remote mountain range in the Pacific Northwest found themselves facing accusations of trespassing after inadvertently crossing onto private property while following a potential Bigfoot track. While their intentions were purely scientific, the lack of proper permission led to a confrontation with the landowner and a subsequent investigation. Although charges were eventually dropped, the incident highlighted the importance of thorough planning and precise navigation when conducting field research in potentially contested areas. Another example, occurring in the Appalachian Mountains, involved a researcher who claimed to have found compelling physical evidence —alleged Bigfoot footprints—on private property. Despite contacting the landowner to inform them of the discovery, the researcher was accused of disturbing the land and was sued for damages. This case underscores the fact that even well-intentioned actions can lead to legal disputes if appropriate permissions and protocols are not followed.

Beyond trespassing, researchers must also be mindful of regulations related to wildlife observation and data collection. Many jurisdictions have laws protecting wildlife, prohibiting the harassment or disturbance of animals, including any attempts to capture, injure, or otherwise interfere with their natural behavior. This is a critical consideration for researchers employing technologies like drones or thermal imaging devices, which could inadvertently disturb wildlife or violate existing regulations concerning their use in specific areas. The use of these technologies frequently falls under the purview of federal, state, or local laws related to aviation, wildlife management, and privacy. Researchers must be thoroughly acquainted with these regulations to ensure compliance. Failure to do so can result in substantial penalties.

Further legal complexities arise when researchers seek to publish their findings or commercialize their research in any way. Copyright and intellectual property rights become relevant when considering the ownership of photographs, audio recordings, and other data collected during fieldwork. If the research is conducted on private land, the landowner may assert ownership over any data collected, creating potential conflicts of interest and disputes over the right to publish or otherwise utilize the collected materials. Similarly, the use of images or recordings depicting other wildlife captured during Bigfoot research must comply with applicable laws, potentially requiring separate permissions and potentially impacting publication strategies.

The complexities surrounding Bigfoot research extend to the potential for misidentification and the subsequent legal ramifications. Cases of misidentification can lead to significant consequences, particularly if the misidentified object is mistaken for a person or an endangered animal. False reports can create panic, waste valuable law enforcement resources, and generate unwarranted fear in local communities. In several cases, reported Bigfoot sightings have led to extensive searches by authorities, diverting resources away from other critical tasks. Researchers must, therefore, maintain the highest standards of scientific rigor, carefully evaluating and documenting all evidence to mitigate the risk of misidentification.

Additionally, researchers should be aware of potential legal liabilities associated with the promotion or commercialization of Bigfoot-related products or services. This could involve the sale of merchandise, guided tours to supposed Bigfoot sighting locations, or the creation of documentaries and other media productions. Such ventures can fall under consumer protection laws, advertising regulations, or even environmental regulations, depending on their nature and impact. Misrepresenting findings, making unsubstantiated claims, or using misleading marketing tactics could result in legal action from consumers or regulatory bodies.

Addressing these issues requires a multi-faceted approach. The development of clear ethical guidelines and best practices within the Bigfoot research community is paramount. A professional organization dedicated to Bigfoot research could play a significant role in establishing such guidelines, providing training to researchers on legal and ethical considerations, and promoting responsible research practices. Transparency and open communication with landowners, relevant agencies, and the public are equally important. Researchers should actively engage in dialogue to address concerns, secure necessary permits, and minimize the potential for conflict.

Furthermore, legal professionals specializing in environmental law, property rights, and intellectual property could provide valuable guidance to researchers, helping them navigate the complex legal landscape and minimize the risk of legal disputes. Such collaborations can ensure that Bigfoot research is conducted in a responsible and sustainable manner, contributing to the advancement of knowledge while minimizing the potential for negative consequences. Ultimately, the future of Bigfoot research hinges not only on scientific breakthroughs but also on a commitment to ethical conduct and legal compliance. By navigating these complex legal and regulatory aspects carefully and responsibly, the field can gain credibility, fostering a more productive and sustainable environment for exploration and discovery. The pursuit of this enduring mystery must be tempered by a respect for the law, the rights of others, and the integrity of the scientific method.

46

FUTURE REGULATIONS AND GUIDELINES FOR BIGFOOT RESEARCH

The ethical and legal considerations surrounding Bigfoot research, as outlined in the preceding chapter, necessitate a proactive approach to developing comprehensive regulations and guidelines. The current lack of formal oversight creates a vacuum, potentially leading to irresponsible research practices, environmental damage, and conflicts with landowners and indigenous communities. A robust regulatory framework is crucial to prevent these negative consequences and ensure the long-term sustainability of Bigfoot research.

The creation of such a framework requires a multi-pronged approach. First, a clear definition of what constitutes "Bigfoot research" is necessary. This definition should encompass a broad range of activities, including field investigations, data analysis, technological advancements in detection and tracking, and the ethical dissemination of findings. This clarity will prevent ambiguity and ensure that all relevant activities are subject to the same standards. The definition should specifically address the use of potentially invasive technologies, such as drones or thermal imaging, and outline the conditions under which their use is permitted.

Next, the establishment of a governing body or committee is

essential. This body could be composed of representatives from various fields, including cryptozoology, environmental science, law, indigenous communities, and land management agencies. This ensures a balanced perspective and avoids bias towards any single approach to research. The committee's responsibilities would include developing and enforcing research guidelines, adjudicating disputes between researchers and landowners, reviewing research proposals, and promoting responsible research practices. Its composition should actively seek diverse perspectives to avoid overlooking significant concerns of the impacted communities.

Guidelines for research permits should be formalized. These permits would be necessary for any investigation taking place on public or private land. The application process should require a detailed research proposal, including a methodology outlining the planned activities, a risk assessment identifying potential impacts on the environment and local communities, and a plan for data management and dissemination. The permit could be subject to specific conditions, such as limitations on the number of researchers, access times, and permitted technologies. Penalties for noncompliance, ranging from fines to permit revocation, should be clearly defined. Transparency in the permitting process is crucial to maintain public trust and ensure accountability. Public access to approved permit applications (with appropriate redactions to protect sensitive locations) would contribute to this transparency.

Further, environmental impact assessments (EIAs) could be mandated for larger-scale research projects. EIAs are routinely used for various developments and could be adapted to Bigfoot research to assess potential environmental effects. Such assessments would include an analysis of potential disturbance to wildlife habitats, the impact of researcher activity on ecosystems, and the use of sustainable practices throughout the research process. The goal is to ensure that the pursuit of Bigfoot does not come at the cost of ecological damage. This approach aligns with increasingly prevalent environmental regulations for various industries and research activities.

Data management and sharing practices should be standardized.

Currently, data collection methods vary greatly among Bigfoot researchers, making it difficult to compare results and draw meaningful conclusions. Standardized data collection protocols would improve data quality and facilitate collaboration among researchers. Furthermore, ethical considerations regarding data sharing and intellectual property must be addressed. Researchers should be encouraged to share their data with the wider scientific community, but they should also be protected from the unauthorized use of their data or findings. This requires establishing guidelines for data ownership, access, and publication, ensuring a balance between open scientific collaboration and the protection of individual researchers' rights. Clear protocols for data storage, archiving and appropriate anonymization should be developed.

The involvement and consultation of indigenous communities is paramount. Many indigenous cultures have rich oral histories and traditions related to Bigfoot-like creatures. Their traditional knowledge can provide valuable insights and perspectives, and their consent is essential for research conducted on lands traditionally inhabited or sacred to their communities. Consultation with indigenous representatives should be mandatory before any research is undertaken in areas relevant to their traditions and land rights. Respectful engagement with these communities, ensuring that their knowledge and perspectives are not exploited, is not just ethically sound; it is also crucial for ensuring the success and legitimacy of Bigfoot research.

Finally, the development of a code of ethics for Bigfoot researchers would enhance the legitimacy of the field. This code could address issues such as responsible land access, data handling, respectful interaction with local communities, and responsible reporting of findings. Adherence to this code would be a condition of obtaining a research permit. This would establish higher standards for conduct and help elevate Bigfoot research beyond the realm of fringe science, contributing towards a more credible and respectable area of scientific inquiry.

The implementation of these future regulations and guidelines will be an iterative process. It will require ongoing dialogue and collaboration between researchers, legal professionals, environmentalists, indigenous communities, and government agencies. However, the longterm benefits of a well-regulated and ethically sound approach to Bigfoot research far outweigh the initial challenges. A responsible regulatory framework will not only protect the environment and the rights of affected communities, but it will also enhance the scientific credibility of the field, allowing for more robust research and a more meaningful understanding of this enduring mystery. The establishment of a clear, well-defined, and fairly implemented regulatory framework will ultimately be pivotal in the future of Bigfoot research, ensuring it remains a pursuit of knowledge rather than a potential source of conflict and environmental damage. Such a framework will attract responsible researchers, deter irresponsible actions, and, perhaps most importantly, help ensure that the pursuit of understanding this elusive creature is both scientifically rigorous and ethically sound.

47

SUMMARY OF KEY FINDINGS AND
ARGUMENTS

This book has explored the enduring mystery of Bigfoot, a creature shrouded in folklore, speculation, and a persistent lack of definitive proof. Our journey began with a deep dive into the historical record, tracing Bigfoot's presence from Native American legends and early European accounts to the surge in modern sightings and investigations sparked by the infamous Patterson-Gimlin film. We examined the purported physical evidence – footprints, hair samples, and vocalizations – critically evaluating the methodological challenges and limitations in their analysis. The inherent difficulties in collecting and preserving such evidence, along with the high potential for contamination and misidentification, were highlighted, underscoring the complexities of proving or disproving Bigfoot's existence.

The contributions of key researchers and investigators, their methodologies, and the ethical considerations inherent in their pursuit were also explored. Their varying approaches, ranging from meticulous tracking to advanced technological applications, revealed a field shaped by both fervent belief and rigorous skepticism. We delved into the contrasting theories attempting to explain the phenomenon, ranging from the relatively straightforward misidentification hypothesis, which attributes sightings to known animals, to more speculative explanations such as the existence of an undiscovered hominid species or a surviving population of an extinct one. The folklore hypothesis, which frames Bigfoot as a purely cultural construct, was also considered, acknowledging its significant influence on shaping the narrative and perpetuating the mystery.

A crucial element of this Investigation was the exploration of the psychological dimensions of the Bigfoot debate. We analyzed the cognitive biases that can influence the interpretation of ambiguous evidence, the role of confirmation bias in reinforcing pre-existing beliefs, and the impact of social and cultural factors on shaping individual perspectives. The psychology of deception and hoaxes was also examined, acknowledging the potential for intentional misrepresentation to contribute to the confusion and complexity surrounding the subject. The book attempted to maintain a balanced perspective, recognizing the validity of both belief and skepticism, and the crucial role of critical thinking in evaluating the available evidence.

The pervasive influence of Bigfoot in popular culture, from literature and film to tourism and merchandise, was also analyzed. We examined how different media representations have shaped public perception, and how the commercialization of the Bigfoot phenomenon has both fueled interest and potentially introduced bias into the narrative. The cultural significance of Bigfoot as a symbol of the unknown, a testament to the persistence of mystery in our world, was also explored.

Looking forward, we examined the potential of emerging technologies to revolutionize Bigfoot research. The application of advanced imaging techniques, environmental DNA (eDNA) analysis, advanced tracking methods, and the burgeoning field of artificial intelligence all hold promise in advancing the investigation. The potential role of citizen science and crowdsourcing in gathering data and expanding the scope of research was also discussed. The ethical implications of utilizing these technologies were carefully considered, emphasizing the importance of responsible data handling and the protection of both human privacy and wildlife habitats.

Finally, we addressed the critical interplay between Bigfoot research, environmental stewardship, and legal considerations. The need to balance the pursuit of scientific inquiry with the protection of natural ecosystems and wildlife was emphasized. Issues of access to public lands, research permits, and data privacy were explored. The existing legal frameworks and potential future regulations for responsible Bigfoot research were also discussed, with a focus on promoting scientific integrity and responsible engagement with the public.

In conclusion, the question of Bigfoot's existence remains unanswered. The evidence, while intriguing and sometimes compelling, remains ultimately inconclusive. While definitive proof continues to elude researchers, the pursuit of understanding this enigma has offered valuable insights into various fields, from investigative techniques to the psychology of belief, and the complex interplay between science, folklore, and popular culture. The ongoing mystery serves as a powerful reminder of the vast unknowns that still exist in our world, and the importance of maintaining a balanced, critical, and respectful approach to investigating the unexplained. The future of Bigfoot research depends on embracing technological advancements, maintaining ethical standards, and fostering collaboration between researchers, scientists, and the public. The enduring fascination with this elusive creature ensures that the investigation will undoubtedly continue, driven by a shared curiosity to uncover the truth behind one of nature's most persistent and captivating enigmas. The book advocates for a continued, scientifically rigorous approach, emphasizing the importance of open-mindedness, skepticism, and a commitment to responsible data gathering and analysis in pursuit of understanding this captivating mystery. The story of Bigfoot, as a creature of legend and scientific speculation, is likely to continue unfolding, shaped by technological advancements and the ever-evolving landscape of our understanding of the natural world. The legacy of Bigfoot, regardless of its ultimate reality, will remain a potent symbol of our enduring fascination with the unknown and our unwavering desire to explore the boundaries of what we think we know. The ongoing exploration of the Bigfoot phenomenon, therefore, transcends the simple question of its existence, becoming a significant lens through which to view our relationship with the natural world, the power of shared narratives, and the human desire to unravel the mysteries that surround us.

The meticulous analysis of eyewitness accounts presented throughout the book has revealed the significant challenges inherent in evaluating subjective experiences. While individual testimonies may hold some weight, their inherent variability underscores the limitations of relying solely on anecdotal evidence in reaching any conclusive determination regarding Bigfoot's existence. The analysis of purported footprints, though demonstrating potential scale and morphology inconsistent with known animals, frequently suffered from issues of verification and the possibility of fabrication or misidentification. Similarly, while DNA analyses have been conducted on purported Bigfoot samples, these results have often been inconclusive, hindered by limitations in sample quality, potential contamination, and the absence of readily available comparative genetic material from a known, similar species. Furthermore, the analysis of vocalizations, while revealing unique acoustic characteristics, has yet to be definitively linked to a specific unknown species, leaving room for alternative explanations such as misidentification of existing animal sounds or human manipulation.

The scientific method demands rigorous testing and verification, and the limitations inherent in the present methods utilized in Bigfoot research necessitate a reassessment of strategies moving forward. This necessitates a cautious approach, acknowledging the potential for both confirmation bias and the undue influence of existing expectations on interpretation of the findings. The book has explored the various facets of this complex subject, from its roots in Indigenous folklore and its evolution into modern popular culture, to the rigorous application of scientific methodologies and the consideration of ethical implications. The multifaceted nature of the phenomenon necessitates that the approach to investigation should remain similarly multifaceted, integrating advanced technologies with critical analysis, and fostering a collaborative approach between researchers, scientists, and the public. The persistent mystery of Bigfoot thus serves not merely as a subject of scientific inquiry but also as a lens through which we examine the processes of scientific investigation, the relationship between scientific data and cultural narratives, and the ongoing debate between belief and skepticism.

The enduring appeal of the Bigfoot phenomenon lies in its ability to transcend the realm of mere biological exploration and enter the wider spheres of anthropology, psychology, and cultural studies. Its longevity as a persistent enigma within our collective consciousness highlights the deeply human inclination to seek answers to the unknown, and to imbue the unexplained with meaning and significance. The story of Bigfoot, therefore, continues to evolve not only in the realms of scientific investigation, but also within the rich tapestry of our shared cultural narratives, where its symbolic resonance far outweighs the definitive resolution of its physical reality. The continued pursuit of understanding the Bigfoot phenomenon requires a nuanced approach that respects both the scientific method and the compelling narratives that have evolved around it, creating a narrative that integrates scientific research and the profound human fascination with the mysterious aspects of the natural world.

48

OPEN QUESTIONS AND UNRESOLVED ISSUES

The enduring mystery of Bigfoot, as we've explored throughout this book, is far from solved. Despite decades of investigation, numerous expeditions, and a wealth of anecdotal evidence, a definitive answer remains elusive. This lack of resolution, however, shouldn't be interpreted as a failure of the investigative process, but rather as a testament to the inherent challenges involved in studying a creature so elusive and enigmatic. The very nature of Bigfoot's alleged habitat – remote, heavily forested regions – presents significant logistical obstacles. Accessing these areas often requires specialized equipment, considerable time commitment, and a high degree of physical endurance. The fleeting nature of sightings, coupled with the often poor quality of visual or photographic evidence, further complicates the pursuit of concrete proof.

One of the most significant ongoing debates centers on the nature of the evidence itself. While numerous footprints, hair samples, and vocalizations have been attributed to Bigfoot, their authenticity remains highly contested. Critics often point to the potential for misidentification, hoaxing, or misinterpretations of natural phenomena. The lack of standardized collection and analysis protocols across various investigations also contributes to inconsistencies and difficulties in cross-referencing results. For example, hair samples collected by different researchers using varied techniques may yield inconsistent results, hampering efforts to definitively link them to a single, unknown species. Similarly, the analysis of footprints requires a deep understanding of geological factors that can influence their formation and appearance. The variability of soil conditions, the pressure exerted by the footprint creator, and even the influence of weather patterns can significantly affect the shape and size of a footprint, making it challenging to draw firm conclusions about their origin. The absence of a readily available 'control' specimen – a captured Bigfoot – further limits the ability of scientists to conduct thorough comparative analyses.

The debate also extends to the interpretation of eyewitness accounts. While many individuals have reported encounters with Bigfoot, these accounts are often anecdotal, varying significantly in detail and credibility. Factors like distance, lighting conditions, emotional state, and pre-existing beliefs can greatly influence the accuracy and reliability of eyewitness testimonies. Moreover, the inherent suggestibility of human memory can lead to inaccuracies or embellishments over time, especially when recounted repeatedly. Researchers have attempted to mitigate this issue through rigorous interviewing techniques and psychological assessments, but the subjectivity of human perception remains a fundamental challenge. The influence of cultural expectations and pre-existing narratives about Bigfoot cannot be overlooked. Many individuals approach the subject with preconceived notions, whether from childhood stories, media portrayals, or established beliefs within their communities. This pre-existing framework can unconsciously shape their interpretations of ambiguous evidence, potentially leading to confirmation bias, where evidence supporting their beliefs is overemphasized while contradictory information is dismissed.

Further complicating the issue is the lack of consensus among researchers themselves. Some investigators adhere to a strictly scientific approach, demanding rigorous evidence and methodical analysis, while others are willing to consider a broader range of evidence, including anecdotal accounts and folklore. This difference in methodological approaches often leads to conflicting interpretations of the same data and fuels ongoing debates. The absence of a universally accepted definition of what constitutes 'proof' further exacerbates these disagreements. Some researchers believe that unequivocal photographic or video evidence is necessary, while others argue that a combination of circumstantial evidence, including footprints, vocalizations, and eyewitness testimony, can collectively build a compelling case. This lack of a standardized benchmark for determining evidence sufficiency contributes to the ongoing uncertainty surrounding the creature's existence.

Beyond the challenges of evidence collection and analysis, the inherent limitations of current scientific technologies also play a role in the continuing debate. While DNA analysis has become a powerful tool in biological research, the low quantity and degraded quality of potential Bigfoot samples often limit the effectiveness of this technology.

Advancements in DNA sequencing technologies could potentially overcome some of these hurdles, but achieving breakthroughs in this area will likely require collaboration across research teams and the standardization of sample collection and processing techniques.

Furthermore, the application of advanced imaging techniques, such as thermal imaging and acoustic monitoring, has the potential to yield new insights. Thermal imaging devices might be able to detect Bigfoot's body heat, even in challenging environmental conditions, and sophisticated acoustic monitoring systems could capture and analyze its vocalizations more effectively. However, the vastness and remoteness of Bigfoot's alleged habitats make the deployment and utilization of these technologies costly and logistically challenging.

Technological limitations also apply to the exploration of Bigfoot's behavioral ecology. While camera traps have become increasingly useful in wildlife research, the elusive nature of Bigfoot makes capturing definitive images incredibly difficult. Even if such images were obtained, understanding Bigfoot's social structure, reproductive behavior, and dietary habits would require extended observation that is practically impossible with a creature so rarely sighted.

The lack of definitive physical evidence has led some researchers to suggest alternative explanations for the Bigfoot phenomenon. These alternative hypotheses range from the misidentification of known animals (such as bears or other primates) to the propagation of elaborate hoaxes. Psychological factors, such as pareidolia (the tendency to perceive meaningful patterns in random stimuli) also contribute to the ongoing debate. This suggests that some purported Bigfoot sightings may be a result of misinterpretations of ambiguous stimuli, rather than actual encounters with an unknown creature.

Despite the challenges and ongoing debates, the pursuit of understanding the Bigfoot enigma continues. New technologies, refined methodologies, and a growing collaboration between researchers are gradually enhancing the field's investigative capabilities. The enduring fascination surrounding Bigfoot, in addition to the potential scientific breakthroughs that its study could inspire, is ensuring a continuation of the quest. Ultimately, the future of Bigfoot research hinges on the ability to overcome the obstacles previously outlined, to refine existing methodologies, embrace technological advancements, and foster a spirit of collaborative investigation that transcends the divides that currently hamper progress. Only through such a multifaceted approach can we hope to shed light on this enduring mystery and gain a clearer understanding of the fascinating creature that continues to occupy the collective imagination. The ongoing debate is, in itself, a testament to the power of the unknown, the strength of human curiosity, and the enduring allure of the unsolved. It is a story that will continue to unfold, one that is enriched not only by the pursuit of scientific truth but also by the compelling narratives and cultural significance it has woven itself into.

49

TECHNOLOGICAL AND METHODOLOGICAL APPROACHES

The persistent elusiveness of Bigfoot necessitates a multi-pronged approach to future research, leveraging technological advancements and refining existing methodologies. One crucial area for improvement lies in the development of more sophisticated remote sensing technologies. Current methods, while useful, often suffer from limitations in range, resolution, and the ability to differentiate between animal and human activity. The deployment of advanced thermal imaging systems with improved sensitivity and range, combined with the use of drone-based aerial surveillance equipped with high-resolution cameras capable of capturing both visible and near-infrared light, could significantly enhance the detection and tracking capabilities of researchers. Integrating AI-powered image recognition software into these systems could automate the analysis of vast quantities of data, flagging potential Bigfoot sightings for human review. This would significantly reduce the time and resources currently dedicated to manual analysis of footage and images.

Furthermore, advancements in acoustic monitoring technology represent another promising avenue for future investigation. The development of sensitive, low-frequency acoustic sensors capable of detecting and recording the sounds produced by large mammals, coupled with AI-based algorithms for sound identification and localization, could revolutionize the way researchers collect and interpret auditory evidence. The creation of a centralized database of verified Bigfoot vocalizations, cross-referenced with sounds from known species, would provide a valuable comparative tool for researchers and greatly enhance the objectivity of auditory evidence analysis. This database would need to account for environmental noise factors and incorporate advanced signal processing techniques to filter out background interference, thereby producing more reliable data sets. Ideally, such a database would be collaborative, accessible to researchers worldwide, and dynamically updated with new recordings and analytical techniques.

Beyond technological enhancements, a critical need exists for refining existing methodologies and promoting collaboration within the research community. Currently, a lack of standardized data collection protocols and variations in the training and experience of researchers contribute to inconsistencies in the reporting and interpretation of evidence. The development of a universally accepted set of protocols for data collection, including standardized methods for documenting sightings, collecting samples (such as hair or scat), and conducting interviews, would greatly enhance the reproducibility and comparability of research findings. This standardization would help ensure that data collected by different researchers can be reliably combined and analyzed collectively. A unified, internationally recognized set of standards would increase the scientific rigor of Bigfoot research, making it more accessible to peer review and scientific validation.

Moreover, promoting collaboration among researchers is essential to advance the field. The current fragmentation of the Bigfoot research community, marked by skepticism, mistrust, and a reluctance to share data, hampers collective progress. A concerted effort to foster a more collaborative and open research environment is crucial. This could involve establishing a central repository for sharing data, developing joint research projects that leverage the expertise of multiple researchers, and creating opportunities for knowledge exchange and networking. Workshops and conferences designed to facilitate the exchange of best practices, methodologies, and data analysis techniques, could encourage mutual learning and address conflicting interpretations of findings. The use of open-source software and data sharing platforms could also significantly improve transparency and promote collaborative analysis of data.

Genetic research offers another promising pathway for future exploration. While efforts have been made to analyze purported Bigfoot DNA samples, the challenges posed by contamination, degradation, and the limited availability of high-quality samples have hampered progress. Future research should focus on the development of more sophisticated DNA extraction and analysis techniques capable of handling degraded or contaminated samples. This may include utilizing advanced sequencing technologies, such as ancient DNA sequencing, to extract reliable genetic information from older samples. A collaborative project focused on the standardization of sample collection and analysis protocols, along with the development of a shared database of genetic information obtained from purported Bigfoot samples, would greatly advance this area of research. This data could be compared against the genomes of known primate species, providing crucial insights into Bigfoot's potential evolutionary history and taxonomic classification.

The development of advanced statistical modeling techniques tailored specifically for analyzing ambiguous and often fragmented Bigfoot data also warrants attention. Existing statistical models may not adequately account for the unique challenges posed by eyewitness testimonies, anecdotal accounts, and inconsistent evidence. Developing sophisticated Bayesian statistical models, for instance, can better handle uncertainty and integrate diverse data types, allowing researchers to quantify the credibility of different hypotheses. The application of machine learning algorithms could aid in pattern recognition within the existing data sets, potentially identifying previously overlooked connections or trends. This might involve analyzing geographic patterns of sightings, correlations between environmental factors and sighting frequency, or identifying subtle patterns in physical descriptions and eyewitness accounts.

Finally, a critical aspect of future research involves addressing the inherent biases and skepticism that frequently accompany Bigfoot investigations. The topic is often fraught with emotional investment and personal beliefs, which can cloud judgment and hinder objective analysis. Future studies should focus on minimizing these biases through rigorous scientific methods, careful control of variables, and transparent reporting of findings. The emphasis should always be placed on rigorous scientific methodology, ensuring that all interpretations of data are based on objective evidence and robust statistical analysis. This may involve incorporating qualitative research methods to further explore the cultural and sociological dimensions of the Bigfoot phenomenon, while simultaneously maintaining a rigorous focus on scientific rigor. This approach requires a commitment to unbiased investigation, a willingness to challenge existing assumptions, and a recognition that not all evidence is created equal.

The enduring mystery of Bigfoot presents a unique challenge, one that requires not only technological innovation but also a renewed commitment to rigorous methodology and collaborative investigation. By addressing the methodological shortcomings, integrating cutting-edge technologies, fostering a more inclusive research environment, and embracing innovative analytical techniques, we can significantly improve our ability to investigate this enduring enigma. Ultimately, the pursuit of understanding Bigfoot is not just about finding conclusive proof of its existence; it's about refining our investigative methods, pushing the boundaries of scientific exploration, and deepening our understanding of the natural world, including its less-understood and potentially unexpected inhabitants. The journey itself, filled with challenges and uncertainties, is a testament to the human spirit's relentless pursuit of knowledge and understanding. And this journey, it seems, Is far from over.

50

SCIENTIFIC RIGOR AND PUBLIC ENGAGEMENT

The pursuit of the Bigfoot enigma demands a sustained commitment to rigorous scientific investigation, a commitment that transcends fleeting interest or sensationalist headlines. The path to understanding, or even acknowledging, the possibility of this creature's existence necessitates a multi-faceted approach. This approach must embrace not only the advancement of scientific methodologies and technological tools but also a crucial element often overlooked: genuine public engagement.

Firstly, the scientific rigor applied to Bigfoot research must be elevated significantly. Past investigations have, unfortunately, been marred by inconsistencies in methodology, a lack of standardized data collection protocols, and an overreliance on anecdotal evidence. Future studies need to adopt a more structured and controlled approach. This means establishing clear and replicable protocols for gathering evidence, including detailed documentation of locations, timestamps, environmental conditions, and witness statements. Crucially, this must extend to the rigorous analysis of purported physical evidence, such as footprints, hair samples, and vocalizations. Advanced DNA analysis, coupled with sophisticated statistical modeling, should become the cornerstone of this evidence analysis.

Furthermore, the scientific community needs to foster a more collaborative and transparent research environment. Sharing data, methodologies, and results openly among researchers, regardless of their individual perspectives, is crucial to building a robust and credible body of knowledge. This collaborative spirit will enable peer review, identifying potential biases, weaknesses, and areas for improvement. The establishment of a centralized

database to collate and manage findings from various research groups could be a significant step towards achieving this goal. Such a database would allow researchers to easily compare findings, identify patterns, and build upon each other's work. This collective approach will not only accelerate the pace of research but also enhance the reliability and validity of the findings.

The limitations of relying solely on anecdotal evidence cannot be overstated. While eyewitness accounts offer valuable insights, their subjectivity introduces a significant source of error. These accounts need to be meticulously evaluated, considering factors such as the witness's perception, memory biases, and the potential influence of preconceived notions. To mitigate these limitations, researchers should adopt rigorous methods for verifying and corroborating evidence. This involves cross-referencing multiple independent accounts, incorporating advanced forensic techniques, and employing psychological assessments of witnesses. Triangulation, a method involving the comparison and reconciliation of information from multiple sources, is another important tool for enhancing the credibility of the research. For example, a purported Bigfoot sighting could be corroborated by physical evidence, eyewitness testimony, and photographic or video footage. The convergence of evidence from independent sources significantly increases the likelihood of a credible finding.

Technological advancements offer a potent arsenal for pushing the boundaries of Bigfoot research. As previously mentioned, sophisticated remote sensing technologies, including advanced thermal imaging systems and high-resolution drone surveillance, can significantly enhance detection and tracking capabilities. The integration of artificial intelligence and machine learning algorithms into these systems could further refine their effectiveness, automating the analysis of large volumes of data and flagging potential Bigfoot sightings for human review. This would free up valuable research time and resources, allowing researchers to focus on the more detailed investigation of potentially significant findings. Beyond aerial surveillance, ground-based sensors, including acoustic and seismic monitoring systems, can detect sounds and vibrations that might indicate Bigfoot's presence. These sensors, when strategically deployed in areas with reported sightings, could provide crucial data on Bigfoot's movement patterns, habitat preferences, and vocalizations. Furthermore, the use of environmental DNA (eDNA) analysis holds immense potential. By collecting and analyzing environmental samples, such as soil, water, or vegetation, researchers could detect the presence of Bigfoot's DNA without the need for direct observation. This non-invasive approach could significantly expand the scope of investigation and overcome some of the inherent challenges in directly observing this elusive creature.

The advancement of genetic analysis is a critical factor. If Bigfoot exists as a distinct species, as some proponents argue, its genetic profile would provide undeniable evidence. Advances in next-generation sequencing technologies allow for the rapid and comprehensive analysis of genetic material, even from degraded or limited samples. This opens up the possibility of identifying unique genetic markers that could distinguish Bigfoot from known primate species. However, the challenges remain immense, particularly in securing authentic and uncontaminated samples. Contamination, accidental or deliberate, could lead to inaccurate results and undermine the credibility of the findings.

However, scientific rigor alone is insufficient. The investigation needs a significant element of public engagement. This is crucial for several reasons. First, it fosters a sense of collective responsibility in the research process. Public engagement, achieved through workshops, educational programs, and community outreach initiatives, encourages people to contribute to the investigation by reporting potential sightings, sharing relevant information, and supporting research efforts. Secondly, it helps to combat misinformation and dispel myths surrounding Bigfoot. Open dialogue and transparent communication with the public can effectively counteract sensationalized accounts and misinterpretations of evidence, fostering a more informed and objective understanding of the subject. The engagement of indigenous communities is particularly vital. These communities have a deep-rooted connection to the land and often possess rich oral histories and traditions related to the possible existence of Bigfoot. Their insights and knowledge should be integrated into the research process, respecting their cultural heritage and traditional practices. The potential for collaborative research between scientists and indigenous communities holds immense value, combining scientific expertise with traditional ecological knowledge.

This engagement should also extend to encouraging a culture of responsible reporting and evidence sharing. It's crucial to combat the spread of fabricated or misrepresented information, discouraging the creation and propagation of "fake news" related to Bigfoot. Educating the public on the importance of responsible data collection and analysis is crucial, fostering a culture of critical thinking and skepticism. This approach will help ensure that the public's understanding of Bigfoot research is accurate and reflects the current state of scientific understanding. The involvement of citizen scientists, trained in appropriate protocols and data collection techniques, can expand the geographic scope of research and enhance the volume of data available for analysis.

In conclusion, the pursuit of resolving the Bigfoot mystery requires a long-term commitment to scientific rigor, technological innovation, and public engagement. By adopting a multi-faceted approach, embracing collaboration, and promoting responsible data handling, we can significantly enhance our understanding of this enduring enigma. The potential discovery of a new primate species, the advancement of scientific methodology, or even the deepening of our understanding of human-wildlife interactions, are all potential outcomes of a renewed and rigorously pursued investigation. The ultimate goal is not just to definitively prove or disprove Bigfoot's existence, but to elevate the quality and impact of the research, ensuring a scientifically sound and publicly engaging investigation of this persistent and fascinating mystery. The journey may be long and challenging, but the potential rewards in terms of scientific discovery and broader public understanding are substantial. The future of Bigfoot research lies not just in the advancement of technology but in the strengthening of collaborative research, transparency in findings, and a dedication to sound scientific principles.

51

CULTURAL IMPACT AND LASTING MYSTERY

The enduring fascination with Bigfoot extends far beyond the realm of scientific inquiry; it has deeply permeated popular culture, shaping narratives, inspiring artistic expression, and fostering a unique community of believers and skeptics alike. This cultural impact is a testament to the creature's enduring mystique, its ability to tap into our primal fascination with the unknown, and its resonance with deeper human anxieties and desires. From the earliest anecdotal accounts passed down through oral traditions of Indigenous peoples to the modern-day proliferation of Bigfoot-themed merchandise, documentaries, and fictional works, the legend has evolved and adapted, reflecting societal shifts and technological advancements. The very ambiguity surrounding Bigfoot's existence allows for a broad range of interpretations and creative expressions, making it a fertile ground for storytelling and artistic endeavors.

Consider the sheer volume of books, films, and television shows that feature Bigfoot or related cryptids. These narratives often explore themes of human interaction with nature, the preservation of wilderness, and the potential consequences of unchecked technological progress. Bigfoot, in these fictional portrayals, frequently serves as a symbol of the untamed wilderness, a powerful force of nature that resists human encroachment and symbolizes the unknown aspects of the natural world. This symbolic representation resonates with environmental movements and contributes to a broader conversation about conservation and responsible stewardship of the planet. Simultaneously, the persistent mystery surrounding Bigfoot's existence fuels speculation and fuels creative endeavors, contributing to a vibrant subculture dedicated to its exploration. The creation of fictional worlds, characters, and narratives built around Bigfoot showcases the creature's power to inspire creativity and to function as a powerful archetype in modern storytelling.

The impact of Bigfoot on popular culture is also evident in the countless pieces of merchandise, ranging from t-shirts and mugs to figurines and artwork, that capitalize on the creature's enduring appeal. The commercialization of Bigfoot, while potentially trivializing the scientific investigation, also reflects the creature's widespread recognition and cultural significance. This commercial success further demonstrates the pervasiveness of the Bigfoot legend in the collective consciousness, turning it into a multi-million dollar industry that caters to both believers and those simply intrigued by the mystery. This economic impact, while indirect, underscores the significant cultural footprint left by the Bigfoot phenomenon.

Furthermore, the Bigfoot legend has played a significant role in shaping certain aspects of folklore and mythology. In many instances, the creature's image is woven into existing narratives, merging with traditional beliefs and lending a sense of timelessness to the legend. This incorporation into existing cultural narratives further reinforces the legend's staying power and its deep roots within specific communities and cultural landscapes. For many, Bigfoot's existence is not simply a scientific question but also a deeply rooted cultural belief, inextricably linked to their heritage and identity. The ongoing discourse surrounding Bigfoot reflects the enduring tension between scientific rationality and the power of cultural beliefs, between the pursuit of verifiable evidence and the enduring appeal of the mysterious and unexplained.

The continuing fascination with Bigfoot, however, is not solely defined by its cultural imprint; it's inextricably linked to the enduring mystery surrounding its very existence. The lack of definitive proof—or conclusive disproof—fuels speculation and keeps the debate alive. This inherent ambiguity is a key factor in its persistent popularity and ongoing cultural impact. The very absence of concrete evidence allows for a continuous reinterpretation of existing data, creating a space for new theories and interpretations to emerge. This persistent ambiguity fuels further research and investigation, perpetuating the cycle of interest and investigation. The enigma surrounding Bigfoot is a self-perpetuating loop of mystery, investigation, and renewed interest.

The mystery of Bigfoot also taps into a fundamental human desire to understand the unknown. It speaks to our innate curiosity about the world around us, our fascination with the unexplored corners of nature, and our inherent drive to seek answers to the unexplained. The creature acts as a focal point for this quest for understanding, drawing researchers, enthusiasts, and the general public into a collective pursuit of knowledge. This shared exploration fosters a sense of community among those who are passionate about unraveling the Bigfoot mystery, leading to collaborative research efforts and information sharing. The online forums and dedicated communities devoted to Bigfoot demonstrate the strength of this collective interest, fostering a unique social dynamic driven by the shared pursuit of a common enigma.

The enduring nature of the Bigfoot mystery also highlights the limitations of scientific inquiry. Despite decades of research, utilizing increasingly sophisticated technologies, definitive proof of Bigfoot's existence remains elusive. This highlights the challenges involved in researching elusive and potentially rare species, as well as the inherent difficulties in collecting and verifying evidence of creatures that may possess an innate ability to evade detection. The challenges faced by researchers serve to highlight the complexity of fieldwork in remote and challenging environments, further fueling the ongoing debate about the methodology used to investigate these types of claims. The limitations of current scientific methods only strengthen the narrative of the enduring mystery, reinforcing the compelling nature of the enigma.

Beyond the scientific pursuit, the Bigfoot mystery has sparked a broader discussion on the nature of evidence, the credibility of eyewitness testimony, and the role of skepticism in scientific inquiry. The debate surrounding Bigfoot has pushed the boundaries of scientific methodology, prompting critical analysis of research design, data collection, and the interpretation of ambiguous evidence. The controversy surrounding Bigfoot's existence has served as a case study for examining the limits of scientific inquiry and the challenges of working within the constraints of incomplete and potentially unreliable data. The inconclusive nature of the Bigfoot enigma highlights the inherent challenges in applying scientific methods to subjects that lie on the boundary of the known and the unknown.

Looking to the future, several potential avenues exist for furthering our understanding of the Bigfoot enigma. The advancements in genetic analysis, remote sensing technology, and advanced imaging techniques offer new possibilities for investigating potential Bigfoot sightings and collecting more robust evidence. The development of more sophisticated camera traps, equipped with AI-powered image recognition, could significantly increase the chances of capturing verifiable footage. The increased accessibility of drone technology opens up new possibilities for surveying remote areas and potentially uncovering new evidence.

These advancements represent a significant leap forward in the tools available to researchers, offering new avenues for investigation and analysis.

In conclusion, the legacy of Bigfoot is multifaceted and complex. It transcends the realm of scientific investigation, impacting popular culture, artistic expression, and even folklore. The creature's enduring mystery lies not only in the lack of definitive proof but also in its ability to tap into our inherent curiosity, our fascination with the unexplained, and our anxieties about the unknown aspects of the natural world. While the scientific pursuit of definitive answers continues, the cultural impact of Bigfoot is undeniable, leaving an enduring legacy that reflects humanity's ongoing fascination with the mysteries that surround us. The future of Bigfoot research lies in embracing technological advancements while maintaining a critical and rigorous approach, acknowledging the inherent limitations of scientific inquiry when facing such an elusive subject. The enduring mystery of Bigfoot, therefore, is not simply a question of whether the creature exists, but a reflection of our ongoing fascination with the unknown and our persistent drive to unravel the secrets that still remain hidden within our world. The continued investigation into the Bigfoot enigma promises further advancement in scientific methodology, technological innovations, and a deeper understanding of human-wildlife interaction, regardless of the ultimate conclusions regarding the creature's existence. The narrative of Bigfoot is not merely a story of a mythical beast; it's a story of human curiosity, scientific exploration, and the enduring power of the unexplained.

GLOSSARY

Bigfoot/Sasquatch: A large, hairy humanoid creature reported to inhabit wooded areas of North America.

Cryptozoology: The study of hidden or undiscovered animals.

Environmental DNA (eDNA): Genetic material shed into the environment by an organism, used for detecting species presence.

Patterson-Gimlin Film: The most famous piece of purported Bigfoot evidence, a short film taken in 1967.

Confirmation Bias: The tendency to search for, interpret, favor, and recall information in a way that confirms or supports one's prior beliefs or values.

ACKNOWLEDGMENTS

This book would not have been possible without the support and contributions of numerous individuals. I extend my deepest gratitude to the researchers and investigators who generously shared their time, expertise, and insights, including [Terry Windell, Gwendolyn Purcell, Bill Rigby, Daniel Benoit, Cliff Barackman, James Faye, Jeff Meldrum,

Rodney Adams, Ron Morehead, Taylor Cook, Dave Groves, Dale Glymph, Jessica Glymph]. Their dedication to uncovering the truth behind the Bigfoot mystery is truly inspiring. Finally, I thank my family and friends for their unwavering patience and encouragement during the long journey of bringing this book to fruition.

ABOUT MICHAEL W. COOK

A seasoned cryptozoologist specializing in the enigmatic Sasquatch, has dedicated over two decades to unraveling the mystery surrounding this legendary creature. Hailing from the dense forests of Eastern Kentucky, Cook has embarked on numerous global journeys in pursuit of answers to some of history's most enduring mysteries. As the original creator of SossSquatch BBQ, he has garnered a dedicated cult following through his passion for cooking and Bigfoot. His extensive resume includes appearances on various television and radio shows, such as Travel Channel's These Woods Are Haunted, I Believe in Bigfoot, and Coast to Coast AM. He is an award-winning chef and reigning champion of many diverse food challenges.

He hosts a weekly podcast, *What's Cookin? w Michael Cook*, found wherever you get your podcasts.

He resides in his home state of Kentucky, where he is a father first and foremost to Peyton, his best friend.

He is proud of his dad who spent 40 years in the coal mines and his mom who worked in healthcare for close to 40 years. Family is everything to Michael, being the youngest of 4. His brothers, Dion (a left leg amputee stemming from a mining accident) and Travis (a physical therapist and grade A nerd) have always had his back. His sister, Christy, is dearly missed and thought about often.

AFTERWORD

Go to hangaripublishing.com to learn more about the Authors and stay up to date with their newest releases.

www.ingramcontent.com/pod-product-compliance
Lightning Source LLC
Chambersburg PA
CBHW061726120626
46550CB00005B/1723